THE BIG SIN

J. Munsettunker.
1982.

For my friend
Jos Collins.

THE BIG SIN

Christianity and the arms race

Kenneth G. Greet

Marshalls

Marshalls Paperbacks
Marshall Morgan & Scott
1 Bath Street, London EC1V 9LB

First published by Marshall Morgan & Scott 1982

ISBN: 0 551 00985 3

Photoset in Great Britain by
Rowland Phototypesetting Ltd
Bury St Edmunds, Suffolk
Printed in Great Britain by
Richard Clay Ltd, Bungay, Suffolk

Contents

Preface

I acknowledge with gratitude permission to quote from the publications referred to throughout the text. If I have inadvertently infringed the copyright of any publisher, I tender my apologies.

My warmest thanks are due to my secretary, Miss Winifred Price, for her kindness in typing the manuscript in the midst of all her other demanding commitments.

Kenneth G. Greet

Westminster, 1982.

Introduction

'Are you the man who described the nuclear arms race as "the big sin"?' My interrogator was a pale, tense-looking man who accosted me on a crowded railway platform. I acknowledged that I had indeed used the phrase at a well-reported public meeting. 'Then you are wrong', came the prompt rejoinder. 'You can't have big sins because you can't have small sins. Sin is sin, and it's against God, and that's that.' Having delivered this piece of instant theology my verbal assailant observed his train approaching and left me as suddenly as he had appeared.

It is just possible that the other party in this brief encounter may pick up this book, and since I have used as its title the phrase to which he took exception, perhaps I should make the reply that his abrupt departure prevented my doing. In any case there may be other readers who have the same reservations.

It seems to me that it stands to reason that, whilst all sins are by definition contrary to the will of God, some sins are comparatively trivial and others are very serious. They are serious because of the degree of wickedness which they involve and because of the appalling suffering which results from their having been committed. In the Sermon on the Mount Jesus Himself seems to suggest that there are degrees of sin (Matthew 5:21–23), and also in His rather mysterious reference to the sin against the Holy Spirit (Mark 3:29) – the one sin for which there is no forgiveness.

However, in defending the title of this book I am not anxious to become involved in a theological altercation which I regard as beside the point. The real point is that we are caught up in the nuclear arms race which is surely the most monstrous madness the world has ever known. It is quite literally madness when the great powers rely for their security on the principle known as MAD – 'mutual assured destruction'. The ever-escalating expenditure on weapons represents a vast wastage of human energy and resource of every kind, and it robs the poor and needy of the chance of a fuller life which could be theirs if we redeployed our wealth away from the production of the machinery of death to the constructive tasks of peace. Far from contributing to our security the proliferation of nuclear weapons has made the world a desperately dangerous place in which to live. Indeed the very future of the human race is in jeopardy.

The arms race, then, is a huge evil which flagrantly breaks the laws of God. It is in a sense the sum of all evils. Christians are called to fight evil in all its forms. But many of the issues with which we concern ourselves, and about which our solemn assemblies pass indignant resolutions, while serious in themselves, are ethical peanuts compared with the big sin which this book examines.

Few issues have moved more swiftly to the centre of public consciousness than this one. There is indeed a gathering momentum of concern all over the world. On radio programmes and in the newspapers, at assemblies and on street corners, voices are constantly heard discussing the questions of peace and disarmament. There is a vast literature and the volume of books and pamphlets increases.

This book is addressed primarily, though not exclusively, to Christians. I do not expect anyone who reads it to agree with all the views expressed, for this is a highly tendentious subject. Nonetheless I believe there is a growing consensus among Christians about some of the things we should be saying and doing. I am anxious to enlarge and deepen the area of debate among us. I believe that there are considerable reservoirs of untapped conviction, but that too many have been inhibited by a frustrating sense of powerlessness. To be sure, there may not be much that one individual can do. But the Christian reaction to that must be: 'then I will do that little as well as I can'. It is moreover true that when men and women resolve to act together much can be accomplished. I believe that, under God, the future depends on a great popular uprising of ordinary people the world over. Only so can the tide of history turn and the long slow journey back from the brink of disaster and towards sanity and peace begin.

If the Christian voice is to be heard, however, we must together study the facts of our current situation. There is no such thing as a Christian judgement on any subject under the sun in default of the facts. The facts of the matter plus a biblical interpretation of the facts: these are the ingredients of a Christian judgement. No amount of unrelated quoting of bible texts can be a substitute for the hard discipline required to enable us to speak out of knowledge. But if the facts are to be illuminated by the truth revealed in the bible, we need the help of the Holy Spirit. Our prayer must be that of Charles Wesley:

'Come, divine Interpreter,
Bring us eyes Thy Book to read'.

In the earlier part of the book we shall try patiently to gather together the facts upon which sound Christian judgement must be based. I cannot claim that the selection and presentation of the facts will be entirely without bias. My comments, like those already contained in this Introduction, are dictated by basic conviction which in turn spring from my Christian beliefs and commitment to Christ. But I shall try to recognize other views where they are held by responsible people.

I am myself a Christian pacifist and have been since as a young man in the years immediately before the last war I had to decide what I believed was my Christian duty. I did not find it easy to come to a decision. The pressures to conform are very strong and most of my Christian contemporaries took a different view. A balanced statement of the pacifist and non-pacifist views will be found on pages 105–107 of this book. The former represents the theology which I accept, but the latter sets out a position which I understand and respect but feel compelled to reject. In my judgement the pacifist case becomes increasingly persuasive as the years go by and Christians face the question 'What is the distinctive contribution that the Church has to make to the current debate on defence and disarmament?' Yet I also believe that in some ways that debate has carried pacifists and non-pacifists together into a new dimension of moral debate and decision-making where many of the old arguments seem rather academic. That is a point which will become much clearer when we reach chapter 7.

Let me now outline the route which we shall take. We begin with the delivery of the first – and so far the only – atom bombs to be exploded over inhabited places, the ones that devastated Hiroshima and Nagasaki in August, 1945. However difficult it may be, we must try to imagine what happened to those Japanese cities and people who lived and died there. We must also try to understand the huge significance of those dread events for the future of mankind.

In the second chapter we look at the development of the nuclear energy industry. We shall be concerned mainly at that point with the production of power for peaceful purposes about which a great debate is raging. But there is a close connection between 'atoms for peace' and 'atoms for war' so we need to try to see the picture whole. Nuclear technology is a highly complex field and the most we can do is to achieve some basic understanding for those of us unfamiliar with the details, avoiding too many technical terms, but also eschewing a merely simplistic view of the issues involved. Having done that we turn in chapter 3 to an examination of some aspects of militarism. Because of the arms race the world has become an arsenal. We look at the way in which nuclear weapons have been developed since the first 'small' atom bomb was dropped on Hiroshima. It is an appalling historical aberration. Chapter 4 contains a brief review of the very inadequate attempts that have been made to achieve a real measure of disarmament. I have already referred to the way in which arms expenditure is virtually a robbing of the poor; chapter 5 indicates how the real enemies of mankind – poverty, hunger, disease and injustice – threaten the lives of millions. Their need adds urgency to all our efforts to redeploy the resources squandered on arms. In chapter 6 I turn aside to deal with what I believe to be a grave distortion of Christian theology which inhibits Christian action for peace. A more substantial chapter addresses the theological questions raised for the Christian by the issues we have examined. Traditional attitudes to peace and war are briefly reviewed and space is devoted to some contemporary and representative Church pronouncements. The final chapter is a reflection on the tasks of the peacemaker today and will, I hope, be found a useful basis for discussion among groups of those who are deeply concerned to make their own contribution to a saner and better world.

1: A peep into hell

'*Here it comes, the mushroom shape . . . like a mass of bubbling molasses . . . it's like a peep into hell*'.

– Sergeant George Caron describing the moments after the dropping of the atom bomb on Hiroshima.

The bombing of Hiroshima

It was a beautiful summer morning in Hiroshima. The date was 6th August, 1945. The sky above was blue and the sunlight seemed to have that quality of golden newness which makes one feel it is good to be alive. By eight o'clock most of the menfolk had left for their work; their wives were clearing up the breakfast things, and from many a home a hum of happiness ascended on the still morning air.

High in the sky above this Japanese city several planes were spotted. The air-raid sirens sounded but nobody took much notice: this was the third alert within a few hours and no bombs had fallen. The morning radio programme reported that the planes appeared to be on a reconnaissance mission.

About 8.15 a.m., however, a small object which looked like a white parachute was released from one of the aeroplanes. It was the first atomic bomb to be aimed at a human target and within seconds it exploded over the city. The plane was called the Enola Gay. It was commanded by Lieutenant Colonel Tibbets. The tail gunner, Sergeant George Canon, observed what happened. He peered down through the bubbling mass of black smoke which rose rapidly to a height of about 50,000 feet, assuming the fearsome shape of a huge mushroom tinged with sinister purple. Far below on the ground fires sprang up everywhere. It was, said the sergeant, like 'a peep into hell'.

The story of Hiroshima has been written up by many, and the terrible testimonies of survivors have become part of the history of the age of terror in which we live. Those able to bear it have seen the horrors reproduced on film. War has always and inevitably involved immense suffering, but the atom bomb introduced into the sad saga of man's self-destruction new and terrible forms of human misery. The bomb was aimed at the centre of Hiroshima, a city of some 400,000 inhabitants. For a distance of two miles in all directions from the centre there was total devastation. Nearly all the city's fire stations were destroyed. Forty-two of the forty-five hospitals were devastated. Such medical facilities as remained were totally inadequate, especially as 270 of the 298 doctors were killed, and 1,645 of the 1,780 nurses.

It is impossible to say exactly how many people died as a result of this one explosion. That fact is in itself a shameful comment on the inhumanity of what occurred. Every soul is precious in the sight of God and every life has a purpose. When we are at our best we recognize this. So the whole world will wait with manifest anxiety for news of the brave efforts of a team of men trying to rescue some little lad trapped on a ledge in a disused mineshaft in a distant land. But in Hiroshima thousands of men, women and children were killed in an instant. The number was probably about 200,000, half the total population of the city. But all kinds of records were destroyed and this alone makes precision impossible.

Many of those who perished were literally turned into cinders, for at the core of the fireball, half-a-mile across, the temperature was an unbelievable 50,000,000 degrees fahrenheit. Even granite melts in a temperature as high as that. The primeval power of the sun had suddenly and terrifyingly descended upon the earth without the benevolent screen provided by distance and atmosphere. The result was rather like what would occur if one directed a powerful blow-lamp onto a nest of ants: suddenly their energetic and purposeful activity would cease leaving only a black mark on the ground.

The immediate physical effects of the atomic explosion were fourfold. There was a blinding flash which blinded some who saw it. Then a gigantic fire. Next came the blast: a roaring tornado of sound travelling at 9,000 miles per hour. Buildings went down like matchboxes crushed by an elephant's foot. But finally came the strange invisible killer known as radiation. Survivors called these destructive rays 'the ashes of death'.

Apart from those who survived with no appreciable damage to health, the fortunate ones were those who died instantly. Little was known among Japanese doctors about radiation and its effects. They could not understand why many people who had no obvious injuries developed a variety of symptoms – bleeding gums, falling hair, fever, vomiting, bloody diarrhoea – and then died. In many ways these conditions were more distressing to deal with than the horrible mutilations and the almost inhuman disfigurements of those who crawled like grotesque automata with their roasted skin hanging in pouches from their bodies. No-one knew how to deal with radiation sickness.

If it is difficult to measure the immediate suffering of the people of Hiroshima, it is quite impossible to grasp the extent of the long-term effects upon them and their children. The psychological consequences of the experience of this apocalyptic event, of wholesale bereavement, of the smashing in an instant of all the familiar structures of life, will be felt for long years to come. The genetic effects of radiation will be seen in children yet unborn. Many children died in the womb because of the radiation from the bomb, and some who came later to birth were badly deformed. Atomic radiation is particularly harmful to young life and to the reproductive cells which are the basic material of new life.

Of all the death-ridden images left on the mind by reading eye-witness accounts of the Hiroshima bombing, perhaps the most haunting is that of the procession of refugees seeking to flee from the wrath that was. There were hundreds upon hundreds of them. Some crawled like animals, so blackened and burned that it was impossible to tell whether they were men or women, young or old; others walked. But all of them moved slowly as if their whole being had been numbed by the narcotic effect of unprecedented disaster. As they moved, their eyes, strangely dull and lifeless, searched among fellow-survivors for the sight of a familiar face, a member of the family. But all were strangers, rendered so by their gross disfigurements. After examining some heap of charred remains, the participants in this latter-day exodus, would continue their meaningless journey. They did not know where they were going, and where they had come from no longer existed. Life itself had lost its significance because all the connections which give it meaning had been destroyed. The all-engulfing black shadow of death had extinguished the light by which we see the way we should go. Some turned back and, like Lot's wife, in the ancient story, were destroyed. Others plodded on but dropped mysteriously and silently in their tracks. Their fellow-sufferers saw them fall but did not seem to understand, for the normal reactions of comprehension and pity had been anaesthetised.

Some of those who have tried to depict what happened in Hiroshima, finding their powers of expression inadequate to the task, have turned to the apocalyptic passages of the bible. Many of these do indeed seem strangely apposite. 'In the days before the flood they ate and drank and married, until the day that Noah went into the ark, and they knew nothing until the flood came and swept them all away' (Matthew 24:38 and 39a). Yet the descriptions of huge flood disasters, still, alas, not uncommon in places like India and China, although they are heart-rending, seem almost to be drawn in black and white compared with the lurid colours which tell the story of a city which melted in a moment of unparalleled terror.

One of the minor effects of the Hiroshima bomb was to stop many of the clocks in the city. That is a fact of great symbolic significance. Next to the unknown date on which Christ was born (or the dates on which He died and rose) the Christian may well judge 6th August 1945 to be the most important date in the human calendar. It marked the end of one age and the beginning of another.

The road to Hiroshima

The bombing of Hiroshima marked the end of one age and the beginning of another in two ways, one minor and one major. It was, in the first place, the culmination of a process of feverish research and technical activity. During the late 1930s it became apparent that before long it would be possible to produce plutonium which is the essential ingredient of a fission bomb. We shall examine the technicalities of the production of nuclear energy and of nuclear weapons in a little more detail in Chapter 2. For the present we are concerned with the immediate background to the fateful event which changed the course of history.

It was Albert Einstein, the famous scientist, who warned President Roosevelt in August 1939 of the rapid developments which might soon lead to the creation of an explosive device of unprecedented destructive capacity. He indicated that research was advancing very rapidly in Nazi Germany. At first the President remained unimpressed by this high-powered intimation. Having been persuaded, however, that it must be taken with the utmost seriousness, he gave orders to begin at once the work necessary to create an atomic weapon. Thereafter the scientists, directed by Julius Oppenheimer, worked under great pressure. Enormous sums of money were diverted to the effort, and, astonishingly, President Roosevelt managed to keep the whole project secret from even his closest political colleagues, including Vice-President Truman. In fact Truman was not informed until the evening of the day when he was sworn in as President following Roosevelt's death on the 12th April, 1945.

Henry L. Stimson, the American Secretary of War, was at pains to point out to the new President not only the enormous destructive potential of the bomb which was soon to be ready for use, but also the political implications of what was being contemplated. In particular he stressed the fact that other countries, including Russia, would undoubtedly follow where the Americans had led. He drew attention to the fact that mankind's technical knowledge had far outstripped advance in moral sensitivity. Prophetically Stimson saw that one of the big questions for the future was how the menace of the nuclear bomb could be limited and controlled. These immensely important long-term considerations were, however, overshadowed by the all-pervading desire of the United States to bring the war with Japan to a speedy conclusion.

Thus it was that the leaders of a Christian nation decided to unleash on mankind a weapon which carried warfare into a hitherto undreamed of dimension of horror. The bomb was dropped on a target deliberately chosen because of its admixture of military and civilian populations. It was known and intended that vast numbers of ordinary people, some of them Christians, would die.

Within the context of military debate and decision it is not difficult to understand why President Truman and his advisers came to the conclusion that the bomb should be used. It appeared to them that Japan was still capable of fighting a long and bloody battle. Her army was more than five million strong. It seemed certain that many hundreds of thousands of Allied soldiers would perish before Japan could be forced to her knees. The choice then appeared to be, as often in time of war, between a greater and a lesser evil.

Looking back, however, on those dread days of decision-making a terrible question has to be asked. Was it, even from the strictly military point of view, *necessary* to drop the bomb? There can be *no* certain answer to that question. Many commentators have expressed the view that Japan was, in fact, on the point of surrender prior to the fateful day when Hiroshima was destroyed. Some say she would have capitulated had the Americans, who were insisting on unconditional surrender, agreed to preserve, as later they did, the institution of the Emperor. It is also argued that it was the entry of Russia into the war just before the dropping of the bomb, that broke the will of the Japanese and forced them to sue for peace. The question whether the use of the bomb was essential to the rapid ending of hostilities will no doubt continue to be variously answered on the basis of conflicting evidence.

The Emperor of Japan wished to surrender as soon as he heard about the extent of the damage done to Hiroshima, but his generals persuaded him otherwise. So on the 9th August 1945 a second atomic bomb was dropped, this time on Nagasaki. It would have been the city of Kokura that suffered devastation but for the fact that weather conditions there were unsuitable for the bombing mission. About 75,000 of the citizens of Nagasaki died. This time the Emperor, asked by the Prime Minister to decide the issue, called for unconditional surrender.

The start of the Age of Terror

If the dropping of the two bombs on Japan marked the end of an age and of a process of scientific/military development, even more significantly it heralded the start of a new age. It is this fact which is of major importance.

The description of our era as a new age is justified by a single fact, namely this: for the first time mankind possesses the power to destroy itself. It is possible to argue that there is nothing essentially new about nuclear weapons. After all, some will say, there has always been violence in the world; once men killed with slings and stones, then with bows and arrows, after that with small guns and larger ones, with little bombs and bigger ones. Yet there is a discontinuity between all that and the state of affairs at which we have now arrived. In all previous ages the destructive forces at man's command have been limited; now in global terms they are unlimited. In the horrible jargon of our time, this is 'the age of overkill', by which we mean that there are enough nuclear weapons to destroy the world many times over. I shall argue later (in Chapter 7) that this quantitative development involves Christians at any rate in the making of new qualitative judgements.

It is important to try to understand the magnitude of the destructive forces now available. This chapter has dealt briefly with the consequences of the dropping of the first two atomic bombs on Japan. By today's standards those bombs were quite small. The destructive capacity of nuclear weapons is measured in terms of kilotons and megatons. One kiloton represents the equivalent of the destructive force of 1,000 tons of conventional explosive TNT. The Hiroshima bomb was was a 12 kiloton weapon and was, therefore, equal to 12,000 tons of TNT. But nuclear weapons are now made in the megaton range, a megaton being the equivalent of 1,000,000 tons of TNT. That is to say, many of the modern weapons, in position and ready to use, are more than a thousand times more powerful than the Hiroshima bomb.

The Hiroshima bomb was a fission weapon. The explosive yield of such weapons is limited because the chain reaction can only be sustained for a relatively short time. Thermonuclear or hydrogen bombs, as they are called, derive their energy from the fusion process and are not so limited. In order to produce the necessary fusion a temperature of about a hundred million degrees centigrade is required. This can be provided only by an atom (or fission) bomb in which such a temperature is achieved at the moment when it explodes. An H-bomb, therefore, includes an A-bomb which acts as a trigger. In this way enormous explosive yields are produced. In 1962, for example, the Soviet Union exploded an H-bomb the explosive power of which was equal to 3,000 Nagasaki bombs. H-bombs are more difficult to make than A-bombs, the problem being to prevent the trigger bomb from blowing the whole weapon apart before enough fusion material has been ignited to produce the required explosive yield.

The following quotation from *Effects of Nuclear War* indicates the likely results of the dropping of a 1 megaton bomb over the Ministry of Defence in Whitehall:

'1 In an area with a radius of one and a half miles, all buildings, including those made of reinforced concrete, would be destroyed and most people would be killed instantly. This would be an area bounded by Bloomsbury, Marble Arch, Sloane Street, and Kennington Oval.

2 In an area with a radius of 4¼ miles, all brick and similar buildings would be destroyed; the clothing of all exposed persons would ignite and they would suffer third-degree burns. This would extend from Holloway to Shepherd's Bush to Balham to Deptford.

3 In an area with a radius of 8½ miles, all buildings would be damaged and half the people would suffer second-degree burns. This would extend from Southgate in the north to Twickenham in the west to Croydon in the south to Woolwich in the east.'[1]

If the bomb used were 20 megatons, the damage described in paragraph (1) would occur in the area described in paragraph (2), and that described in (3) would extend to a radius of over 23 miles – as far as Welwyn, Maidenhead, Gatwick and Gravesend.

Facts such as these lie behind the solemn warning of distinguished men like Earl Mountbatten of Burma. Not long before he was murdered by terrorists off the coast of Ireland he made a speech which has since been widely quoted. In it he said: 'As a military man who has given half a century of active service I say in all sincerity that the nuclear arms race has no military purpose. Wars cannot be fought with nuclear weapons. Their existence only adds to our perils because of the illusions which they have generated.

'There are powerful voices around the world who still give credence to the old Roman precept – if you desire peace, prepare for war. This is absolute nuclear nonsense and I repeat – it is a disastrous misconception to believe that by increasing the total uncertainty one increases one's own certainty.

'The world now stands on the brink of the final Abyss. Let us all resolve to take all possible practical steps to ensure that we do not, through our own folly, go over the edge.'[2]

Like many others, Lord Mountbatten had taken a peep into hell, and longed to see mankind find the way of deliverance. The world had entered upon the age of terror.

The atomic bomb was the latest demonstration of the astonishing new powers released from the Pandora's box of modern science, part, in fact, of the great energy revolution which is the subject of the next chapter.

2: The great God 'K'

The two worlds of man – the biosphere of his inheritance, the technosphere of his creation – are out of balance, indeed potentially, in deep conflict. And man is in the middle. This is the hinge of history at which we stand, the door of the future opening on to a crisis more sudden, more global, more inescapable and more bewildering than any ever encountered by the human species and one which will take decisive shape within the lifespan of children who are already born.

Barbara Ward

The energy revolution

The great pryamids of Egypt, standing like silent sentinels on the edge of the desert, are massive monuments to the skill and energy of those who built them long, long before Christ was born. The skill is revealed in the precise cutting of the huge stones which fit together with scarcely a paper thickness of space between them. But it is the energy of which one thinks with a certain awe. Thousands of men sweated and toiled, and not a few died, and when at length the task was finished every ton of stone had been hoisted into place by their own muscle power or that of the animals they employed.

How different life is today. With the comparatively recent arrival on the scene of the internal combustion engine a new age began. Now man was able to harness the forces of nature and use them vastly to extend his own mobility and efficiency. Tasks which once took years could now be completed in days, and, with the rapid advances in the applied sciences, range upon range of new achievements, hitherto undreamed of, came within his grasp. The incredible fact is that the vast majority of the goods in use today have been invented in my life-time. In terms of technical achievement nearly everything that ever happened has in fact happened in this century. The journey from the past into this amazing era is, in respect of the welter of scientific ideas and their practical applications, rather like moving from the lonely acres of Salisbury Plain into the turmoil of Piccadilly Circus in the rush hour.

The results of all this have been far-reaching. The whole pattern of life has been changed: where men live, how society is organised, and what men expect of life. Those of us who live in the affluent parts of the world now take for granted the complex array of facilities which are ours to command: transport, public services of every kind, sophisticated entertainment, a communications network which brings the world into our parlour, and labour-saving gadgets in abundance. All of this is attained with the use of less and less physical human energy, and correspondingly more reliance on the power produced from a variety of fuels. Perhaps the most dramatic illustration of this is the fact that when a man travelled to the moon it took no more of his own physical energy to accomplish the actual journey than he would have expended on a comfortable day's holiday ramble. The rest of the power needed to propel him to his destination was provided by the fuel in the rocket.

During this period when suddenly all the graphs of human material progress have soared through the ceiling, world population has risen at an unprecedented rate. This is Noah's new flood – of people. There are now more than 4,000 million of us and by the turn of the century that number will probably have reached 6,000 million. The picture, then, is one of more and more people with ever-increasing expectations. The hungry millions in what we have learned, a little ambiguously, to call 'the developing countries' look longingly at their more wealthy neighbours, and, not surprisingly, want to catch up.

The implications for both present and future of this situation are many, varied and interrelated. A world in which rich and poor are so painfully divided is bound to be a place of tension and conflict. The problems of population control, food supply and environmental pollution are now part of the familiar kaleidoscope of global concern reflected in endless public conferences and popular debate. Some parts of the many-sided problem are easier to tackle than others. Finding enough food adequately to feed the vast global family presents a gigantic challenge both in respect of more efficient production and more effective and equitable distribution. But food supplies are renewable: as the bible promises, seed-time and harvest do not cease. More intractable problems confront us in the related fields of raw materials and energy production. Here we have been drawing to a large extent on finite and therefore exhaustible stocks.

Our limited resources

It is only in comparatively recent times that the wealthy members of our affluent western society have awakened to the fact that there are not unlimited supplies of everything. It has come as a considerable shock to those who have accepted without question that an ever-expanding economy is normal and desirable to have to recognize that there are limits to growth. Some of the materials of which we make the most extravagant use will undoubtedly be exhausted within a measurable period of time. Copper is an example. Next to iron and aluminium copper is used more than any other metal, yet copper is comparatively scarce. Zambia supplies most of the copper we use in Britain; indeed half the government revenue of that African State and over 90 per cent of its export earnings come from the sale of this metal. Obviously the future of the copper industry will greatly affect the economy of Zambia, but equally the exhaustion of the supply of this much-used commodity will require all kinds of adjustments to the industry and technology which at the moment rely upon it.

Stewardship of God's gifts

Our particular concern in this chapter is with the energy problem. Christians approach this, as they do all the related issues to which I have referred, from the basis of certain convictions. They believe that this is God's world, and that He has revealed His loving purpose, for all His children. We are the stewards of His good gifts and must use them in the service of others, especially the poor and needy. Any suggestion, therefore, that science is in itself an evil thing, is incompatible with a Christian understanding of man and the universe. Pure science is the search for truth. The God who created all things is Himself the source of all truth. The scientist, therefore, in so far as he uncovers truth, is 'thinking God's thoughts after Him'. When, however, we consider the application of scientific truth to the daily life of man then other forms of truth become important. Before we can decide whether any particular application of scientific knowledge is to be approved or resisted we have to ask questions about the purpose of life and the rights and wrongs of various proposals. In other words religion and morality, which are other ways of searching for and discovering truth, have to play their part in determining how we should proceed.

The nuclear energy debate

One of the most obvious examples of the way in which science, religion and morality all become involved in a single issue is the present debate about nuclear energy. To state the matter in its simplest and most obvious form: nuclear energy can be used for the benefit of mankind – for example, to provide electricity to light and heat our homes; or it can be used to destroy a city like Hiroshima, bringing untold misery to thousands. Stated thus the issue seems simple enough. The Christian approves the right use of this new form of energy and condemns the wrong use of it. In fact, howwever, as we all know, this monumental statement of the obvious does not get us very far. Supposing it can be shown that, terrible as they are, in a fallen world like this nuclear weapons are the only effective deterrent to potential aggressors and therefore the only safeguards of peace, what moral judgement does that line of argument dictate? That is a question to which we shall turn later in this book. In the meantime we have to note that there is another area of debate concerned with the peaceful uses of nuclear energy. Does the production of this form of energy not expose us to unacceptable hazards? Is there the possibility, because of environmental pollution, of our ending up with a poisoned planet no longer capable of supporting life? In short, are the gains of nuclear advance outweighed by the dangers and disadvantages?

Here we are confronted by one of the crucial questions of our time. To attempt a snap answer would obviously be foolish and invite the proper contempt of those who have been at pains to try to gather the material for an informed and responsible judgement. We must at least attempt to indicate the kind of evidence that has to be considered.

For many people there is a psychological barrier to be breached before this exercise can begin. The whole discussion of nuclear energy is shrouded for them in dark mists of fear and dread. Not only is there the knowledge of what happened when the first atomic bombs fell, but there are ugly rumours of the havoc wrought by atomic radiation from nuclear power stations. Lacking any understanding of what is evidently a highly complex subject, some people tend to close their minds and turn away from further contemplation of the subject.

The nature of nuclear energy

The first point, then, that must be made clear is that when we talk about nuclear energy and about radiation we are discussing natural phenomena. The sun, upon which our very life depends, is a giant nuclear reactor. The earth on which we live almost certainly had its origin in a physical sense in a nuclear explosion within a larger mass in one corner of the unimaginably vast universe of which it is an infinitesimal though highly significant part. Plutonium from which nuclear energy is produced was present in the earth at its formation. It does not now occur naturally because over a long period of time it decays to the substance known as uranium. But the earth is full of radioactivity and always has been: there is nothing new about that.

Before we attempt an answer to the question about the relative risks and advantages of man's development and use of nuclear energy we must attempt, as simply as the subject will allow, to explain the way in which this energy is produced and the principles underlying the process.

Most of the electricity we use in our homes comes from generators housed in power stations. The turbines which produce the electrical current are powered by steam. The heat required to turn water into steam comes from burning coal or oil. Essentially then the process is one whereby the energy of the sun stored up over long periods of time in these fossil fuels is converted first into heat, then into the rather mysterious form of energy known as electricity, and thereafter back again into heat (as in the electric fire) or light (as in a lamp) or some other form of energy (as in a mixing machine).

In the production of electricity in a nuclear power station the heat required to drive the generators is derived from uranium. To acquire a rudimentary understanding of how this is done we need to know a little about atoms which are the tiny basic building blocks out of which everything we touch is made. We now know that an atom consists of a nucleus containing even smaller particles called neutrons and protons. Around these even smaller particles move: these are called electrons. Some elements have atoms with more than one kind of nucleus and these have different numbers of neutrons. Elements of this kind are said to have several isotopes. Some isotopes of heavy atoms split in two when another neutron hits their nucleus. When this happens they are said to undergo nuclear fission and this is a process which releases a great amount of heat.

Every time a neutron hits a nucleus between one and three neutrons are released. In a nuclear reactor these neutrons are used to create still more fissions thus bringing into being a chain reaction. When the American scientists who worked on the production of the first atom bomb finally perfected the method of creating this chain reaction they called it the 'K factor' and some of them nick-named it 'the great god K' because of their awareness of its enormous potential.

The fuel used in thermal reactors is uranium. Only some of the isotopes of uranium can undergo fission – mainly those known as uranium – 233 and uranium – 235. Natural uranium contains only 0.7% uranium – 235; all the rest is uranium – 238 which is not capable of fission. But in fast reactors more fissile material is produced than is actually used up. They do this by converting uranium – 230 into plutonium – 239 which is a very good nuclear fuel. Hence the reason why such reactors are called 'breeders'.

In the coming years we are likely to see further rapid developments in the scientific research relating to nuclear energy. Nuclear fusion, as distinct from fission, is a technique which may be capable of opening up vast new sources of primary energy. The prospects of this are succinctly stated in one of the papers produced in preparation for the Conference on Faith, Science and the Future held at the Massachusetts Institute of Technology in the U.S.A. from the 12th to the 24th July 1979 and convened by the World Council of Churches:

'Following some thirty years of research (started in the 1950's) there is the expectation that, within the next ten years, the scientific feasibility of a fusion device with an energy producing plasma will be demonstrated. This demonstration would not, however, be in any real sense an engineering prototype of a commercially acceptable device. This further step presents formidable technical, economic, and engineering problems. While one can say therefore that a fusion energy device can be built, one can only speculate on its cost and commercial feasibility. It is likely that it would be costly compared to present nuclear installations and may be a large device. A fusion reactor produces significant amounts of new radio-active material in its structure and releases large amounts of tritium. While the amounts of radio-activity are indeed much less than those involved in fission reactors and the half lives are shorter, there will still be the need for radio-active waste management programmes. The excess neutrons in a fusion reactor can also be used to breed fuel for nuclear fission reactors. Fusion will therefore have environmental problems of its own.'

Radiation and the element of risk

We now come to the important fact that all the materials involved in the production of nuclear power are radioactive, that is their atoms are unstable and change spontaneously into atoms of another material. In this process they emit rays, which, in varying degrees, are harmful to life. This radioactivity diminishes with the passage of time in accordance with a law of geometric progression. The activity diminishes by one half over a certain period known as its 'half-life'. If the period is one year then at the end of twelve months the activity will have been reduced to a half, after two years to a quarter, and so on. Most of the radioactivity from the nuclear waste produced by reactors disappears within a year or two but plutonium – 239 has a half-life of 24,000 years.

It is possible to measure the amount of radiation received by living cells. The unit of measurement is called a sievert (sv). A single dose of 10 sv. would almost certainly cause a man to die within a few weeks. Much smaller doses however, can cause cancer, and damage to the reproductive organs which lead to abnormalities which may be transmitted to succeeding generations. Many of those who died as a result of the Hiroshima explosion did so because of exposure to a very large dose of radiation and not because they were either burnt or blasted.

Jim Garrison, in a much discussed book entitled 'From Hiroshima to Harrisburg'[4] traces the history of nuclear power from the developments which led to the making of the Hiroshima bomb to the incident in the nuclear reactor at Harrisburg, Pennsylvania, U.S.A. in 1979 which, Garrison alleges, came very near to being a national disaster. Thousands of people were temporarily evacuated from their homes because it was feared that the reactor had run out of control and might explode. The sub-title of the book is 'The Unholy Alliance' and the thesis is that just as the use of atomic power to blast a city to ruins was a scandal which humanity should not have tolerated, so also the development of that same power for peaceful purposes is so fraught with potentially disastrous consequences that this way of solving our energy crisis should be abandoned.

Garrison's narrative is indeed an impressive one and constitutes a most solemn warning to look with critical care at what we are doing and where it may take us, though his central thesis has been severely criticised. At the end of his survey he presents his conclusions which I quote in full (pp. 203–4):

'1. At each stage of the fuel cycle radioactive effluents are *legally* released into the air and water. This is because of the acceptance of the *threshold theory* which asserts that a human body can sustain 'safe' dosages of radiation. Without the acceptance of this theory, nuclear facilities could not be built, for radiation releases are inevitable.

2. All recent studies indicate that there is no such thing as a

safe level of radiation exposure. *Any* radiation is potentially harmful whether naturally occurring or human made. This is why around nuclear facilities of all sorts – from mines, to mills, to conversion plants, to enrichment plants, to fuel fabrication facilities, to nuclear reactors, to reprocessing plants, to nuclear weapons factories, to waste disposal sites – both the *workers* in these facilities and the *public* living around the facilities are experiencing dramatic increases in cancers, in leukemia, and in genetic defects. There is no such thing as a 'safe' nuclear reactor or facility any more than there is such a thing as a 'safe' nuclear weapon.

3. Because of the high toxicity of the radioactivity produced and because of the extremely long half-lifes of many radioactive agents – strontium-90, 28 years; radon-222, 80,000 years; plutonium-239, 28,000 years – the damage to human life and environment will not stop with our generation. Rather, each nuclear facility, while itself only lasting thirty to forty years, produces radioactivity which will live on long after both the builders of the plant and the plant itself are gone and forgotten. Our generation, therefore, is producing a radioactive legacy that will contaminate the environment and damage human life for thousands of generations to come.

4. There is at present no *place* to store radioactive wastes and no *technology* known which is capable of containing the long-term high-level wastes for as long as they must be completely isolated from the human and natural environment.

5. If the nuclear fuel cycle was stopped, the present loss of life and the prospect of leaving a radioactive legacy to future generations could be largely avoided.'

There can be no doubt whatever that the production and development of nuclear energy involves very real risks. But are the risks as great as Garrison alleges and are they, comparatively speaking, so grave that informed and responsible citizens should band together in opposition to the whole misguided venture?

It goes without saying that there is nothing which makes it always and inevitably wrong to take risks. On the contrary it may often be right to take risks. Humanly speaking we can assert that God Himself takes risks. The incarnation was, one might say, 'a calculated risk'. When Jesus said (Mark 8:34)

'Anyone who wishes to be a follower of mine must leave self behind; he must take up his cross, and come with me', He was surely saying that life for the Christian is in one sense a very risky business. On the other hand, there are unjustified risks: actions which are foolish and irresponsible because, even if they produce some good, it is clear that this will be altogether outweighed by the evil that will result.

What, then, is the extent of the risk involved in the production of nuclear power? Can the risk be justified and is it possible to take a less sombre view of the matter than that adopted in the book by Garrison? We need also to ask whether, even if the risks are justified, the production of nuclear power can solve the energy crisis either in terms of the amount that could be generated or the cost effectiveness of the methods that have to be used. Are there other options open, and, for that matter, to what extent is the 'energy crisis' the result of man's sinful propensity to waste precious resources, or fill the world with complex and, in terms of human happiness and fulfilment, unnecessary gadgetry?

The risks involved in the production of nuclear energy for peaceful purposes were carefully examined by an expert working party set up under the aegis of the Methodist Church. The report entitled 'Shaping Tomorrow'[5] and dealing with a number of aspects of modern technology was written by an editorial group led by Mr. Edgar Boyes, the Vice-Principal of the Luton Industrial College. It distills the results of a number of consultations extending over two and a half years and involving some sixty scientists, technologists and engineers. We will examine what it says.

Examination of the risks

a) *Routine Operations.*
The risks arise from a number of different factors. First there are those which arise from the routine operations of the nuclear power industry. A body called The International Commission on Radiological Protection (ICRP) has recommended that governments should ensure that no member of the public should ever receive more radiation than the 'maximum permitted dose' (MPD) which is reckoned to be 5 milli sv. in any one year. It is asserted that if a person were to

receive that amount every year for eighty years the risk of cancer induced by radiation would be about 1 in 200. It must, however, be noted that the risk of contracting cancer in the ordinary way during such a period of time is about 1 in 5, that is forty times greater.

The average dose of radiation received by members of the public as a result of the nuclear industry is estimated at 2.2 micro sv. per year. This is about 2,000 times smaller than the MPD and is, in fact, 500 times smaller than the amount we receive from the natural background. The dose received by those who actually work on nuclear sites may be twelve times as much as that to which the rest of us are subject, but it is still far below the MPD.

Much has been made of the fact that the reprocessing plant at Windscale in Cumbria discharges water containing radioactive wastes into the Irish Sea thus contaminating the fish which people eat. Tests and research show, however, that the risks arising from this are still well within the level of reasonable safety. The writers of 'Shaping Tomorrow' conclude: (page 20):

'The risks even to the most exposed members of the public from the routine operation of the British nuclear industry are thus small. To the average person they are negligible and even collectively they do not amount to more than about one or two cancers per year. Moreover, they mostly come from caesium discharges from Windscale, which are caused by a corrosion problem with Magnox fuel which is already being dealt with and should not occur with the next generation of reactors. The average individual risk of death to people in Britain from the present nuclear industry is therefore about 1 in 36 millions per year, three times less than being struck by lightning, 4,500 times less than being killed in a motor car accident and about half-a-million times less than dying of disease. The nuclear industry in Britain will probably grow 3–10 times, generating about 50% of our electricity instead of 12% as now. However, because of the present dominant contribution to radioactivity release of caesium discharges from Magnox fuel the total radioactivity released and consequent risks are unlikely to rise.

'We do not have comparably precise knowledge of the total risk associated with coal burning-power stations, apart from the risks in coal mines. Coal stations emit very large quantities of poisons like sulphur dioxide and also cancer producing chemicals like benzpyrene; studies suggest that about 100 times as many cancers are caused as by the comparable generation of nuclear electricity.'

b) *Accident.*
The second source of risk is the possibility of accident. Quite serious accidents have occurred like the one at Harrisburg so dramatically written up in Garrison's book. A very thorough theoretical study was undertaken in the U.S.A. by Professor N. Rasmussen and a team of researchers. Their estimate was that there was a risk of 1 in 100,000 per reactor per year of an accident big enough to cause at least 10 cancer deaths over the following 10–20 years. These calculations refer to thermal reactors and no similar research has yet been done on fast reactors where the results of accident might be greater even though the risk of such catastrophes may be less.

A large and extremely serious accident at a nuclear power station is not impossible, though unlikely. Again, however, it must be remembered that we are talking about *comparative* risks. Dams have occasionally burst with heavy loss of life to those caught in the flood, but no-one on that account argues that no dams should ever be built. The annual deathrate through accident in British coalmines is about 25 per hundred thousand. More than 6,000 people die annually on the roads of the U.K. The conclusion of 'Shaping Tomorrow' (p. 21) is:

'Given the smallness of the risk of large nuclear accidents and their dispersed impact there seems to us no good reason to let them dominate the discussions of nuclear power. Nuclear electricity is almost certainly safer than that derived from coal. We believe that all lives should be held at least approximately equal so that it would be wrong to choose an overall more dangerous technology because media coverage and public interest in large accidents makes an overall safer one with very rare but large accidents seem unacceptable.'

c) *Waste Disposal.*
Next we consider the risks arising from the disposal of nuclear waste. This waste material is not only radioactive but

also emits heat over a long period. The intention of the nuclear industry is to store the liquid waste in containers for a period of 10–20 years and then to turn it into ingots of glass. These will then be put into metal shells in water-filled ponds before final burial either in a stable rock formation or under the deep bed of the sea. The purpose of the protective coverings and the burial beneath the ocean is to prevent contamination of the water which we drink. The problem about stable rock formations which are completely dry is that earthquakes might bring about changes in the earth's crust and the seepage of water which, if the insulation around the nuclear waste decayed or were punctured, could affect rivers, lakes and inshore waters.

In spite of cries of alarm from some environmentalists 'Shaping Tomorrow' concludes (p. 21):

'Several detailed studies, for example in Sweden, have estimated the dose members of the public are likely to receive from waste disposal. For example, even if people drank only water from a well near the waste repository their dose from the waste would probably never exceed 1% of the natural radiation dose.'

A similarly reassuring note was sounded by Dr. Walter Marshall, chairman of the United Kingdom Atomic Energy Authority. He said that Britain 'has produced only enough high-level radioactive waste from nuclear power stations to fill two semi-detached houses and it should be stored above ground for at least 100 years before disposal. By the end of the century the amount of highly active waste would only amount to the size of two swimming pools' he added. 'As a result of the industry's work on sealing liquid atomic waste in glass the amount of radiation was "trivial" compared to that in a nuclear reactor.'[6]

d) *Misuse by terrorists*.

Terrorism is a much-publicised fact of life today and the ingenuity of terrorists is all too obvious. It is natural, there-fore, that people should ask: 'If terrorists can hijack aero-planes and use every kind of explosive device to accomplish their ends, what could they not do by exploiting the materials which are used in the nuclear power industry?' It would be foolish to deny that there is here proper ground for concern.

The main consideration, however, is the danger inherent in the toxic substances themselves which makes the handling of them, especially by those not well-informed and properly equipped, an extremely hazardous business.

'Shaping Tomorrow' concludes (pp. 22 and 23):

'The growth of nuclear power will certainly provide the terrorist with new opportunities, but they will be difficult and in many ways unrewarding compared with the many others already available to him. Unfortunately, at the present time they would have tremendous publicity value, far out of proportion to the real threat they pose.

'In summary, there is good scientific evidence that the physical risks of nuclear power are small. The industry has been examined by a great many regulatory institutions, far more carefully than any other industry, to ensure its operations are reasonably safe. Perhaps the most convincing evidence of its good safety record is to compare fatal and other accidents for nuclear installations (power stations, fuel manufacture and reprocessing plants, UKAEA labs, etc.) with those for a variety of other industries. We believe that the individuals and society should be willing to accept these small risks, provided they are purposeful and bring benefits enabling people to lead fuller lives.'

The plutonium economy

There is one other prospect which has caused a good deal of anxiety to those who gaze into the nuclear crystal ball and try to read the future. Because of the transport and use of highly dangerous materials, and particularly because some of those materials can be used to make atomic weapons, the whole industry is necessarily subject to close surveillance and is surrounded by barriers of secrecy. This is the kind of situation in which basic human liberties can all too easily be eroded. The tendency is for those who are entrusted with the task of maintaining security to be given (or to seize) more and more power over their fellows. Freedom of political expression, especially if it is critical of established policy, is frowned upon and then curbed.

The threat to human liberty contained in the development of the plutonium economy is a particularly clear example of a very much wider problem caused by the ever-increasing complexity of our modern society. Simply stated it is this: how can ordinary people play any part in the decision-making processes of the nation, when such decisions have to be made, and can only be made, by those few with expert knowledge of the issues involved? The problem looms even larger when we consider the fallen nature of man, and realize that so often decisions made by the few on behalf of the many are dictated by those with vested interests.

The only safeguard against corruption of the kind referred to is constant vigilance. Christians need to be as well-informed as possible. The appointment by the Churches of specialist groups of their own helps in the general process of education and vigilant examinations of trends and policies. Public hearings, such as those organised by the British Council of Churches, are an admirable expression of Christian responsibility and an effective means of education. In December 1976 the Council invited a number of national bodies and certain expert witnesses to submit 500 word statements on particular aspects of the matter. Twelve submissions were received from British Universities. A panel of people with expertise in various aspects of nuclear energy were recruited and they cross-examined the witnesses on their submissions for a total of ten hours. Members of the public were invited to participate by sending in written questions. The Report[7] of this hearing provides a body of information which is of great value to individuals seeking to reach an informed judgement.

Economic considerations

Decisions about whether or not to develop the nuclear power industry cannot be made in an economic vacuum. As we noted earlier, cost effectiveness is an important aspect of the whole debate. There are many items that must be included in the balance sheet which determine the cost per unit of electricity produced by using nuclear fuel. For example, in addition to the direct costs of production there is the very considerable expenditure on basic research, on the disposal of radioactive wastes and on decontamination processes. Christians with their deep sense of responsibility for the wise

37

stewardship of God's gifts will recognize this economic question as being also a moral question. How we spend our money, both personally and nationally, is a matter about which we have to give account before our Maker.

To state the obvious, money spent on excessively expensive methods of energy production cannot be spent on other things like schools and health services. The impact of fuel costs both upon the economic health of a nation and upon its social and cultural life is seen all too clearly in the the recession which has dominated the news for several years past. The price of oil has shot up dramatically with the result that the economies of all the nations that depend upon that commodity have been severely affected. Not only that, but the attempts of the big powers to secure their access to the world's rich oil fields has exacerbated international tension.

According to the annual accounts and Report (1979–80) of the Central Electricity Generating Board the comparative cost of electricity produced in nuclear power stations has been reducing. For the year 1979/80 the costs per unit were: nuclear – 1.30, coal – 1.56 and oil – 1.93. The Board predicts the following comparative costs in the future for power produced by stations in the process of building: nuclear – 2.4, coal – 3.6 and oil – 6.9. These figures cannot be more than a rough guide since there are any number of variables which could affect them in the future, such as building costs and changes in the price of the basic fuels required to drive the generators.

Most of the nuclear power stations so far built are located in the wealthy nations for the obvious reason that they are expensive to construct and require a high degree of technical skill and efficiency to run. It could be argued, and indeed is argued by some, that in developing the nuclear power industry the rich nations are only widening the gulf between themselves and the poor parts of the world. Just how great that gulf is in energy terms can be seen from the following striking quotation:

'The use of energy in the world is grossly unbalanced. The consumption of energy per head in industrialized countries compared to middle-income and low-income countries is in the proportion of 100:10:1. One American uses as much commercial energy as two Germans or Australians, three

Swiss or Japanese, six Yugoslavs, nine Mexicans or Cubans, 16 Chinese, 19 Malaysians, 53 Indians or Indonesians, 109 Sri Lankans, 438 Malians, or 1072 Nepalese. All the fuel used by the Third World for all purposes is only slightly more than the amount of gasoline the North burns to move its automobiles.'[8]

The demand for more energy by the developing countries is bound to increase, for energy is one of the basic requirements for more rapid development. In the poorest countries far too much wood is used as fuel. Indeed almost half the world's wood yield is burnt as fuel. Deforestation leads to soil erosion and flooding; cattle dung which should be used as soil fertiliser is also burnt as fuel. The richer nations have a responsibility to help the poorer improve their energy supplies. This means exploring every method of producing energy and of reducing dependence on the limited supplies of fossil fuel which one day will be exhausted.

The last sentence of the quotation above from the Brandt Report indicates the enormous dependence of the rich nations on oil for driving cars and the public vehicles which are used on the roads. So far nuclear power in terms of its peaceful deployment has been used exclusively to produce electricity. A large part of the energy crisis, however, is caused by the ever-increasing need for portable liquid fuels. Any hope, therefore, that even the very rapid building of more nuclear power stations could provide an early solution to the energy problem is doomed to disappointment. Are there, then, other options open to us?

Other options

There are various schools of thought about how the world is to solve the problem of the ever-increasing demand for energy. Some take the extreme view that we should abandon the production of nuclear power. They place very great stress on the negative factors some of which have been referred to in this chapter. Their view is supported by many who have not studied the issue in any detail and who, perhaps, have allowed their minds to be so influenced by the horror of nuclear weapons that they are not able to give the question the dispassionate analysis it requires.

This approach to the problem is also strongly advocated by those who see the way ahead as being that of 'the soft path' to increased energy production. According to this line of thinking we have not yet begun to realize the immense resources of renewable energy available from nature by harnessing the power of winds and tides and by direct utilisation of the energising rays of the sun. Anyone who has visited a great hydro-electric installation such as the one at the Volta Dam cannot fail to have been impressed by the giant turbines turned by the rushing force of the water falling through huge pipes. The deep power-filled humming sound remains in the ear long afterwards as a testimony to the gigantic potential of nature when its forces are trapped and controlled.

The soft energy path is bound to make an immediate appeal to all those with a deep concern for the environment. The pollution of the biosphere is one of the concomitants of our highly industrialised and technological society which is the cause of ever-increasing anxiety. Many of the world's lakes and rivers have been poisoned to an alarming degree, and the marine life in the sea is threatened in a number of areas by pollutants of various kinds. The air is similarly affected: the effects of lead poisoning from petrol fumes is only one example of a growing problem of considerable complexity.

There is no doubt that the future will demand much greater exploitation of the soft energy resources of the earth. Nearly all the energy of wind, tide and sun is in fact wasted. Enough solar energy reaches the deserts of Saudi Arabia to equal the entire global reserves of oil, gas and coal. Any simplistic dream, however, of solving all our problems by a vast proliferation of solar roof panels, windmills and hydro-electric plants must be brought into touch with reality. The proposals further to exploit soft energy resources must be subject to the same technical, economic and other tests as plans relating to the future use of fossil fuels and nuclear power plants. Economic considerations are vitally important. Not nearly enough is known as yet about the comparative costs of producing electricity from renewable energy resources on a very large scale. Such estimates as have been attempted suggest that the cost is likely to be considerably greater than for nuclear power. Neither must it be assumed that soft energy technology does no damage to the environment. The wholesale harnessing of tides could slow down the rotation of the earth with significant effects on the length of the day and the rhythm of the seasons.

Most governmental agencies concerned with energy planning and strategy claim that all options must be pursued.

The W.C.C. Conference on Faith, Science and the Future referred to earlier reflected the deep concern felt all over the world by those who realize the momentous nature of the decisions that have to be made. The most debated of all the recommendations considered by that Conference was the one which proposed a moratorium on the construction of all new nuclear plants for five years. The intention of this was to encourage 'wider participation in a public debate on the risks, costs, and benefits of nuclear energy in all countries directly concerned'. This recommendation was carried on a divided vote: 129 for, 45 against and 21 abstaining. A similar division of opinion was registered in different parts of the world. Some thought the Conference had gone too far, others that it had not gone far enough. Others again said that a moratorium of the kind suggested would be unjust in that it would allow nations with nuclear reactors under construction to enlarge their nuclear capacity while denying nuclear energy entirely to other nations. Nevertheless the Central Committee of the W.C.C. later endorsed this recommendation.

The same Conference rightly and inevitably turned its attention to the grave issue of the connection between nuclear energy programmes and the prospect of the proliferation of nuclear weapons. I shall refer to this more fully in chapter 7. For the present it must be clearly recognized that there is an intimate connection between 'atoms for peace' and 'atoms for war'. The horrific weapons which could destroy the world and the energy programmes which are increasing in number all the time depend in large part on the same underlying scientific discipline, engineering and laboratory capabilities.

At every turn of the road decisions have to be made. Most important of all is the decision whether or not we are going to incline towards a nuclear energy economy. A responsible Christian approach must insist on the importance of sound education on the details of the issues that have to be considered, and sustained dialogue between those empowered to make decisions and those who are affected by their decisions.

The need for economy

Ours is without doubt the most wasteful age in history. The fact is demonstrated on every hand. Jesus told the story of Lazarus and how the poor man fed off the crumbs that fell from the rich man's table (Luke 16:19–31). It is not the crumbs on the floor that worry a sensitive visitor to many a well-appointed restaurant, but the large helpings of good food that are left on the plates of those who order or are provided with much more than they either need or want. In the poorest parts of the world it is a touching sight to observe the way in which an old tin can is treasured and used as a receptacle for water; but in the wealthy west the average family throws away more than 500 tin cans every year and each individual uses up an average of eighteen tons of material annually. Vance Packard quotes an extreme example of 'the throwaway spirit'. In the U.S.A. many potato peelers are lost through being thrown away with the peelings. A firm producing these culinary tools decided to colour the handles to look as much like a potato peeling as possible, thus ensuring that even more were lost. Because the colour was not attractive to the eye of the purchaser the peeler was pinned onto a brightly painted card.

It is, however, in relation to our squandering of energy that the need for economy has made the greatest impact on public consciousness. Energy conservation is now a booming business. And not before time. In most Western European countries half the energy generated is wasted. Heat is allowed to escape from badly-insulated houses and inefficient industrial plant. The massive cooling towers which are dotted about our cities have been described as 'cathedrals of idiocy'. If one stands by any city bus-stop during the rush hour one sees a constant stream of cars carrying the driver and no passengers. We have become accustomed to living in an age when we switch everything on and then forget to switch it off.

The Christian concept of stewardship has a compelling relevance to the situation outlined in this chapter, and those who preach it may claim as allies the increasing number of agencies, from government departments to organisations like 'Friends of the Earth', who trumpet the need for responsible care of the planet and its bounteous though limited resources.

3: The mildew of militarism

The nuclear arms race has helped to transform the world into a potentially more perilous place than it has ever been in all human history.

Lord Zuckerman

All-pervasive militarism

At the end of a period when we had been excessively busy for months on end my wife and I spent a week in Paradise. Through the kindness of friends we visited a remote Pacific Island. The sun shone from clear blue skies. The long ocean rollers crashed onto the white sands, and we walked alone on the palm-fringed beaches far from the crowds and the incessant demands of our London life. From the window of the lovely house in which we stayed we looked across the bay, beyond the coral reef, to a green headland with an unusual and bewitching shape. We thought we would go to explore it, but the local people told us it was out of bounds. It was occupied by the military, like a quarter of that sea-girt jewel. So does the mildew of militarism leave its ugly mark on the brightest and the best. Beneath the hump of the hill fearsome weapons were stored: part of the vast American arsenal.

Take a closer look at the lovely Island of Oahu. The bus will take you right round it comfortably in a day for 25 pence. It is the headquarters of the U.S. Pacific Command and the hub of American military activities for more than half the world's surface – probably the largest unified military operation on earth. The famous Pearl Harbour provides maintenance facilities for nuclear powered submarines and Oahu with the other Hawaian Islands is of strategic importance to the Pentagon. Among the military activities on the Islands are mid-ocean repair facilities for ships and aircraft, training on 'the largest shooting gallery in the world', communications stations, navigational aids, anti-submarine warfare equipment, ammunition supplies, research into aerospace technology, space-watching systems, military intelligence and checking of arms sales (the U.S. being the largest supplier of arms in the world).

The casual visitor to Oahu might easily be deceived into thinking that nothing unpleasant could ever happen in so idyllic a spot. But with the Pearl Harbour ordnance docks capable of handling up to four million pounds of explosives at a time accidents are bound to happen and they do. In 1944 an accidental detonation of ammunition killed over 500 people. In 1969 a suspected rocket accident triggered an explosion which killed 24 and injured nearly 100 on the aircraft carrier Enterprise. There have been many other accidents in the area of Hawaii and there is much local concern about the effects of the discharge of radioactive liquid wastes and of low-level radiation. This is the dark side of Paradise.

We have become accustomed to the acceptance of a military framework to life. Many of those who occupy the chief posts in the world's governments are military men. Many of them gained power and hold onto it – often very precariously – by the use of military force. Much of the history of our own beloved country is written in blood. Even in peacetime we cannot mount any big national occasion without the aid of the military, and the great ones of the land parade before us in uniforms bedecked with medals.

No-one will deny that many of those who fought and died on battlefields, in the air or at sea, displayed great courage. Many of our military leaders have been men of noble spirit and high ideals, with a passionate love of their country. Whatever may be said about the past, however, the fact is now that war involves such a degree of hideous and senseless slaughter that all right-thinking people must want to see it outlawed for ever. Whatever glory may have been thought to attach to individual participation in the military defence of the realm, we now face a situation in which there is no defence, and the resort to war – now a monstrous mechanised madness – might be the last bankrupt act of a dying race.

Yet no amount of rhetoric, however pacific in intention, will move us very far along the road to peace. The mildew of militarism is a long-established growth. Its removal can only come about when millions of people the world over are converted to the view that enough is enough, and that there is a better way. That work of conversion is essentially that of the Holy Spirit, the living Presence of Him who is the Author of peace and Lover of concord. But part of the task of peacemaking to which Christians are called by God consists of patient publishing of the facts, the education of the mind and conscience of society.

We look now, therefore, at some of the facts about the cost of the world's military enslavement, the part played by the arms trade, the way weapons are deployed, recent changes in military strategy and the involvement of Great Britain.

The cost of militarism

The military machine is a voracious consumer of wealth, and unbelievably extravagant. The stockpile of nuclear weapons in the world now exceeds 50,000. They possess more than a million times the destructive power of the Hiroshima bomb, or more than three tons of TNT for every human being in the world. The U.S.A. and the U.S.S.R. are investing over one hundred million dollars per day to upgrade their military arsenals. The U.S.A. spends twice as much each year on training military personnel as is spent on 300,000,000 school-age children in Southern Asia. The newest military tanks consume 1.9 gallons of fuel per mile. World expenditure on arms exceeded $460 billion in 1979. In real terms this is about four times the amount that was being spent on armaments annually at the end of the last world war. Tragically, some of the steepest percentage increases in arms expenditure have been in developing countries.

The number of people directly employed by the world's military establishments is vast and ever-increasing. There are now about 25 million in the regular armed forces of the nations, 7 million more than in 1960. To that huge total must be added at least a further 50 million paramilitary and reservist forces. If we add the number of those employed in weapons research and production or similar activities, then the number on the pay-rolls of the world's defence ministries exceeds 100 million.

Even if one accepts the view that in a fallen world like this military preparedness is essential to national security, it must surely be as clear as day to anyone who looks squarely at the facts that the great military juggernaut has run out of control. The world's arsenals are grossly overstocked. Most pathetic of all is the race between the U.S.S.R. and the U.S.A. to achieve parity and then superiority. The race continues long after both sides have amassed sufficient explosive strength to blast each other out of existence. They have led the world into the age of over-kill.

It requires only a little commonsense to trace the connection between this prodigal expenditure on armaments and the global economic and social tensions which constantly provide the gloomy headlines in all our newspapers. Not, of course, that political leaders often allude to this connection. Instead they talk endlessly of their enemies abroad against whom it is essential to arm to the teeth. Thus they deflect the attention of the public they are supposed to serve away from the real problems with which they should be grappling, and obscure one of the major causes of the malaise that threatens the stability of national structures and institutions.

Another aspect of militarism that helps to explain its persistent hold on humanity is its creation of privilege and power bases. The recent history of Africa provides many examples of the way in which military solutions are sought for political problems. All too easily this becomes the accepted norm, and so the military and political establishments become inseparable. With the growing hold of the military on the political machinery of a country inevitably secrecy increases (under the pretext that security demands it), and accountability decreases. So the road from democracy to dictatorship is trodden hard by the heavy boots of the military.

The cost of militarism in economic and social terms is serious enough, and its bearing on the real struggle which should be engaging all our energy and resources will be considered in the next chapter. But worst of all is the cost in human lives. More than twenty million people have died in armed conflict since the end of the last world war. Between one and two million of these died in the Vietnam War. That disastrous conflict cost the U.S.A. 300 billion dollars.

America used 13 million tons of high explosives (more than six times the weight of bombs dropped by that country during the whole of the Second World War), and American forces delivered 90,000 tons of gas and herbicides. It is perfectly true that the existence of military weapons cannot be regarded as the sole cause of the wicked wastage of human life which war involves. The causes of conflict lie deep in the heart of man and the corporate life of nations. But the spread of militarism exacerbates all the occasions of conflict and encourages the view that human problems can be solved by resort to violence when, in fact, most problems are only thereby increased.

A further comment on the increasing cost of militarism is made by Norman F. Dixon in his study of Military Incompetence.[10] He does not set out to attack the armed forces as such or to condemn the majority of senior military commanders. He does, however, examine some of the military blunders of the past which have proved distressingly costly in terms of lives lost. He recognizes the increasing complexity of modern methods of warfare and suggests that less able people are now being recruited to undertake more difficult tasts. If that is the case, the implications are grim.

Dixon makes the following comment on recruitment for the armed services:

'The gap between the capabilities of the human mind and the intellectual demands of modern warfare continues that expansion which started in the eighteenth century. It is probably opening from both sides. While modern war becomes increasingly swift and deadly, and the means by which it is waged increasingly complex, the intellectual level of those entering the armed services as officers could well be on the wane. This tentative supposition is based on the fact that fewer and fewer of the young consider the military to be a worthwhile career. One has only to look at contemporary recruiting advertisements to realize the evident difficulties of finding officer-material. They spare nothing in their efforts to convince an unresponsive youth. The services are depicted as glittering toyshops, where handsome young men enjoy themselves with tanks and missles while basking in the respect of lower ranks hardly less godlike than themselves. In their eagerness to drum up applicants these calls to arms attempt the mental contortion of presenting the services as a classless society in which officers nevertheless remain gentlemen. The clear implication of such expensive pleading can surely be only that the market for a military career is shrinking, to say the least. To meet this fall-off in officer recruitment insufficient has been done, in the writer's opinion, to improve the real as opposed to the advertised incentive-value of a military career'.[11]

Dixon gives four reasons for pursuing the study of military ineptitude:

'The first is that military organizations may have a particular propensity for attracting a minority of individuals who might prove a menace at high levels of command, and the second is that the nature of militarism serves to accentuate those very traits which may ultimately prove disastrous. In theory, then, errors of generalship could be prevented by attention to these causes.

'Thirdly, the public has, at least in the democracies, some real say as to who should make its political decisions. This control does not apply to generals. Even the *worst* government and *most* inept prime minister come up for possible dismissal every so often. This is not true of armies and navies. We may have the governments we deserve but have sometimes had military minds which we did not.

'Fourthly, if one of the main differences between military and political organizations is in the degree of public control, that between the military and commerce lies in decision pay-offs.'[12]

Before we leave the subject of the cost of militarism something must be said about the specious argument often heard that disarmament would seriously increase our already massive problem of unemployment.

No-one needs any persuading of the seriousness of the unemployment situation. Facts and figures quoted from reliable sources in 'World Military and Social Expenditures 1980'[13] show that there are now more people unemployed than at any time over the past twenty years. In industrial countries the average rate of unemployment doubled between 1970 and 1980. The International Labour Office estimates 455 million jobless or underemployed in developing countries (not including China and other centrally planned Asian countries).

Comparative statistics clearly indicate that the higher the rate of military expenditure, the lower the growth of productivity. Ruth Sivard comments:

'Military budgets are dead-end expenditures. They do not foster growth. Through their inflation-inducing effects and the economic uncertainties to which they contribute, they inhibit the capital investment essential for development. Through their drain on research funds and talent, they restrain the productivity gains which could open markets and ensure more jobs across the board.

'Military expenditures are in competition with other government budgets which do a considerably better job of creating employment opportunities. Non-defence needs tend to be less capital-intensive, more labour-oriented. Official calculations for the U.S. economy indicate that, for the same expenditure of funds, up to twice as many people can be employed in schools, health services, building homes and transit systems, as through military budgets. As an increasing number of developing societies have also found, defence spending is the least efficient road to nation-building and the job opportunities needed for rapidly growing populations.'[14]

People sometimes ask why it is that Germany and Japan – two nations that suffered defeat in the last war – seem so prosperous now compared with Britain. A large part of the answer is that Germany for a crucial period after the war, and Japan until now were prohibited from spending their resources on armaments. Thus they were able to devote their industrial muscle to the creation of peaceful and profitable enterprize.

In the light of this, it is astonishing how many people still cling to the notion that the military machine is a great boon in terms of employment. It is almost as absurd as saying that the more infectious diseases we can spread around the greater will be the job opportunities for doctors. Even some Christians who read the prophetic words of Isaiah (2:5): 'They shall beat their swords into mattocks and their spears into pruning-knives', seem incapable of grasping the fact that the redeployment of our resources is possible. It is within this context that the word 'conversion' has come to have a profoundly important industrial meaning. Trade unions in Britain, West Germany, the U.S.A., Italy and Sweden have expressed their interest in attempts to redeploy for peaceful purposes the resources used in the production of armaments. Leaders in this field are Lucas Aerospace and Vickers. Mary Kaldor comments on the specific example of Lucas Aerospace and on the general point that such initiatives can make a significant contribution to disarmament and peace:

'The Lucas Aerospace workers have actually achieved some success in pressing their management to undertake the manufacture of socially useful products. For the first time, workers are inserting their own criteria, as both producers and consumers, into the choice of products. They are, in a sense, developing a new mechanism for conversion, which, if it spreads, could change the composition of power in existing institutions – local councils, regional development councils, the Industrial Manpower Commission, the Atomic Energy Commission, for example – and which could eventually be embodied in a new set of planning institutions which set priorities according to the social needs of consumers and which guarantee stable, although mobile, employment.

'Any campaign for disarmament must join forces with workers in the defence industry in demanding conversion. Conversion – along with other more traditional disarmament issues – could build upon the growing fissures within the armament system and direct current frustrations towards disarmament rather than war. It could help to initiate a process of conversion which would *precede* disarmament. Conversion would thus be seen as a way of achieving disarmament rather than a thorny problem to be solved after the politicians had finally willed the reduction of armaments. Conversion would not just be a matter of turning swords into ploughshares. It would be a matter of creating a new mechanism for the wider process of economic conversion, matching the desperate needs of the modern world with resources that are either misused or not used at all. It could thus undermine the political and economic basis for armaments in advanced industrial countries and it would help to overcome the structural problems, weaknesses and divisions of different economic systems. Hence it could help to remove the causes of war.'[15]

If the process described by Mary Kaldor is to gain momentum there is another area in which conversion becomes essential, and this brings us nearer to the meaning which Christians commonly attach to the word. The fact is that weaponry still has a fascination for many people. How otherwise are we to account for the popularity of films and television programmes which depict scenes of battle – blazing guns, roaring tanks, and planes and ships with names like 'Tiger' and 'Avenger'? Arms and fighting make a particular appeal to the aggressive components of the male psyche. Some recent studies of the distressing incidence of the crime of rape have suggested that the motivation of the rapist is not so much that of sexual gratification in the more obvious sense as of desire to demonstrate male dominance over women. It is an interesting reflection that this line of thought is borne out by the linking of the two words 'Sex Pistols' in the title of a singing group. If a literary and historic reference were needed to explain what many might regard as an inexplicable association of words, it might be found in William Langland's *Piers Plowman* (1377): 'While thou art young and thy weapon keen, wreak thee with wiving'.

What is needed is the conversion of the common understanding of the essence of maleness to that which lies at the heart of Christianity. Christians believe that in Jesus Christ the world has seen the perfection of manhood. His invincible strength, however, was not expressed in aggressiveness but in that superb control which enabled Him in the face of fierce opposition and cruel taunts to keep silence (Matthew 26;63. 'When He was abused He did not retort with abuse. When He suffered He uttered no threats'. (1 Peter 2:23).

It is perhaps worth noting in this context that some Protestant Christians, in their desire to dissociate themselves from what they see as excessive devotion to the Virgin Mary in Roman Catholicism, have failed to appreciate the importance of giving her a proper place in the drama of man's redemption. In the glorious words of the Magnificat Mary sings in revolutionary terms of a reversal of the false ideas which have so often led the world close to disaster when they have been made the springs of human action:

'The arrogant of heart and mind He has put to rout,
He has brought down monarchs from their thrones,
But the humble have been lifted high.' (Luke 1:51-2)

In practical terms the conversion of the military outlook to that of the peacemaker must be set forth in terms which are exciting, demanding and creative. The search for a sane society and a civilised environment must be expounded as what William James called 'the moral alternative to war'.

The arms trade

In view of the astronomical expenditures on arms, it is clear that the arms trade is thriving; it is also immensely lucrative. In the judgement of the present writer it is the most cynical and unprincipled trade the world has ever seen. That is a harsh judgement and it will no doubt be resented by some. They may point out that this is an industry which provides millions of people with well-paid jobs, furnishes nations with the essential means of caring for their security, and out of its profits contributes much to charity; moreover some of those who hold commanding positions in the industry have been heaped with honours and are very amiable fellows. All of which is entirely beside the point. The firms that produce armaments are in business to sell their wares to anyone who will buy them. There is not the slightest doubt that the arms trade has expanded its market by fomenting trouble and playing off one side against another: Saudis against Iranians, Israelis against Egyptians, Greeks against Turks. It thrives on espionage, secrecy, bribery and the most scandalous elements in international relationships.

Governments are, of course, involved in arms deals and not infrequently justify their activities by claiming 'We only sell to friendly countries'. It is a hollow claim. On the rapidly changing chessboard of international politics, countries that are friendly today can become ill-disposed tomorrow. Here are some interesting examples of the 'boomerang' effects of military deals and aid:

'Egypt received $4 billion in Soviet military aid before switching to the U.S. as principal arms supplier. In 1979-80,

Soviet arms previously supplied to Egypt turned up in Afghanistan in the hands of rebels fighting Soviet forces.

'Yemen received $400 million in emergency western arms aid during its 1979 war with communist South Yemen. In 1980 Yemen turned to the U.S.S.R. for Mig fighters and tanks, and edged toward a merger with its communist neighbour.

'Iran, whose Shah had been the best customer of all for U.S. arms (including $900 million in military gifts), had his regime toppled in a revolution armed with 300,000 weapons looted from government arsenals.

'China and the U.S.S.R. had a falling-out in mid-1960 and Soviet technicians were abruptly withdrawn. Among other forms of aid, U.S.S.R. had supplied China with nuclear information. The two communist giants now face each other with nuclear missiles over a tense border.

'Vietnam received China's military aid until 1978, when it became a member of Comecon and heavily dependent on Soviet aid. In 1979 China invaded Vietnam, facing some of its own arms in a short but bloody war.

'Ethiopia, the largest recipient of U.S. arms in Africa ($244 million in gifts) and thanks to them a modern military power despite an abysmally low level of national income, staged a revolution in 1974 which brought a Marxist government to power. Ethiopia became a Soviet ally.

'U.S.S.R. is now making use of the large naval bases in Vietnam constructed by the U.S. during the Vietnam War.

'U.S. is negotiating with Somalia to occupy the Berbera base which the U.S.S.R. constructed before Somalia and U.S.S.R. parted company in 1977.'[16]

Equally deserving of criticism is the defence sometimes offered by those who say 'If we don't sell arms, others will.' Exactly the same excuse was made by supporters of the slave trade. Yet Britain, at that time a great power, took the lead in abolishing a hateful trade. As has already been said, the curbing of the arms trade presents formidable difficulties, but it is not impossible. The economic ramifications of the subject are complex. The arms-producing nations have argued that only by exporting weapons can they develop their own technology and retain their own potential for war. When one line of business has run out great steel firms have turned to arms production to maintain their momentum. This is what happened to the Krupp, Vickers and Carnegie undertakings. When the great railroad companies had completed their network of communications in the industrialised countries the demand for steel slumped badly. So the firms producing it turned to the manufacture of arms – a booming and inventive industry providing numerous outlets for expanding trade. In the early 1930s Britain was far and away the biggest exporter of arms in the world.

In the aftermath of the First World War there was great indignation directed against those who had made money out of the misery of war. The British parliament discussed the nationalisation of the arms trade. In 1935 a Royal Commission was set up to enquire into the arms business. It sat for a year and during its hearings, held in public, there were fierce arguments between representatives of the armaments firms and those opposed to their unfettered activities. In the end, however, the Commission concluded that 'the reasons for maintaining the private industry outweigh those for its abolition'.

Public attitudes changed significantly after this as the clouds of war began again to darken the horizon. The government initiated a programme of rearmament, the order books of the arms dealers filled up, and unemployment decreased. But by the end of the war the weapons of conflict had become immensely more sophisticated and relied less on heavy industry, as in the past, and more on an alliance between pure science and light industry. Moreover, because of the vast sums required for research and development governments became more deeply involved in finding finance and making decisions. The centre of the world's armaments industry moved away from Britain and Germany to Russia and the U.S.A.

In the next chapter we shall look at some of the efforts that have been made to reverse the now once again spiralling arms race. For the present we note the important judgement of Anthony Sampson:

'The arms business has always insisted that it is like any other business, with no special moral responsibility, and the complexity of modern weapons makes it all the easier to forget their ultimate purpose. The involvement of governments has encouraged arms salesmen to delegate any misgivings; but the governments deliberately conceal the full extent and implications of the trade, for fear of arousing public opinion and "left-wing extremists". Yet informed public opinion, in spite of the old spell of weapons, can often by wiser and more moral than governments operating in secrecy.

'The problems of arms may be more complex, and their control more difficult, than the layman might at first imagine; but the ordinary citizen is right in thinking that the arms trade, like narcotics or slavery, is different from other trades. The more the public is informed and involved, the more prospect there will be of achieving a saner world.'[17]

The nuclear inventory

We know that the U.S.S.R., the U.S.A., the U.K., France and China have nuclear weapons. We can't be sure whether any other countries, such as South Africa or Israel, possess them. It is undoubtedly true that a number of other countries which possess nuclear installations could rapidly produce nuclear weapons, if they chose to do so. Most of these countries (Argentina, Brazil, India and Pakistan, as well as South Africa and Israel) have not ratified the 1970 Non-Proliferation Treaty.

Anyone who regularly reads a newspaper will see frequent references to the various kinds of weapons which fill the bursting arsenals of the two super powers. The references are often highly technical and the use of initial letters tends to confuse the average reader. It may be worthwhile to attempt a brief and simple (and therefore inevitably incomplete) description of the main categories of nuclear weapons presently available for use. It will be convenient to concentrate on the U.S.A. because from the outset America has been and still is several years ahead of the Soviet Union in the technology of nuclear weaponry. The U.S.A. has about 50% more warheads (more than 9,000 in all) in its strategic arsenal than the Soviet Union, but their total explosive power is reckoned to be less than those of Russia. The Soviets have tended to concentrate on intercontinental ballistic missiles and submarine launched ballistic missiles with much less emphasis on long-range bombers. It is usual to distinguish the big 'strategic' weapons from the smaller 'tactical' weapons. In the former class there are three main kinds of delivery system: the inter-continental ballistic missile (ICBM), the submarine-launched ballistic missile (SLBM), and the long-range bomber.

1. *Strategic weapons*
   a) Intercontinental Ballistic Missiles.
   Minuteman Mark II has a speed of 14,000 mph and a range of 7000 miles. Its single warhead is 125 times the size of the Hiroshima bomb. There are 450 of these.
   Minuteman Mark III This is a more advanced version of the Mark II with a range of 8,000 miles. It carries three warheads each with a power of 350 kilotons. It can be fired to fall within 300 yards of its target. There are 550 of these.
   Titan Mark II This is America's largest ICBM with a speed of 17,000 mph, a range of 9,300 miles with a single warhead 750 times as powerful as the Hiroshima bomb. There are 52 of these.
   A new ICBM is being developed which will carry ten 350 kiloton warheads. It is suggested that each missile will have 23 different launching sites so that a potential enemy would never be sure at which target to aim if he were minded to undertake a first strike.

   b) Submarine-launched Ballistic Missiles
   Polaris submarines are 400 feet long and weigh 6,000 tons. They carry 16 missiles each and these travel at 6,600 mph with a range of 2,875 miles. The U.S.A. now has ten of these submarines still in service.
   Poseiden is larger than Polaris and carries about ten missiles each rated at 40 kilotons. It has roughly the same range as Polaris but greater accuracy of aim. There are 28 of these.
   Trident Mark I is larger again with a longer range of 4,600 miles and carries eight 100 kiloton weapons. The U.S.A. plans to have 12 of these vessels in service by March, 1982.
   Trident Mark II This missile is expected to become operational in 1987. It will have a range of 7,500 miles, twice the firing power of Trident Mark I, and much greater accuracy.

c) Strategic bombers

Boeing B52 Stratofortress This very large eight-engined long-range jet bomber came into service in 1955. About 750 were built at enormous cost. They were designed to deliver H bombs over their targets – as was done at Hiroshima. Because such planes are vulnerable to anti-aircraft defences, planes have been developed which carry missiles which can be launched a long way from the target. Some 5,000 of these are likely to be produced. There is as yet no Soviet equivalent of these planes.

2. *Tactical weapons*

The U.S.A. has a large variety of smaller nuclear weapons and systems designed for limited 'theatre' warfare. (The use of terms throughout this dismal catalogue is an interesting revelation of the military mind which is capable of infinite ingenuity in inventing euphemisms to obscure the real horror of what is being described). The particular 'theatre' most often discussed is, of course, Europe. The tactical arsenal contains, among other things, nuclear depth bombs for use against submarines, atomic demolition charges for blowing up bridges, roads and installations, and nuclear-capable artillery.

Changes in military strategy

In all the areas referred to developments and modifications are constantly being undertaken and introduced. It will be clear that the trend is always in two directions: more effective destructive capacity, and greater accuracy in attack. Since so much has been made in expositions of the doctrine of deterrence of the idea that nuclear weapons will never be used, it must be noted that one of the major reasons for the search for greater accuracy of aim is to enable a country which is, or believes itself to be, under threat to knock out the enemy's weapons on the ground before they can be used in attack. Hence the emergence of the sinister phrase 'a pre-emptive first strike'. This is a point which will be of particular importance when we come to reflect on the moral implications of military developments.

The Reagan administration in the U.S.A. has revived a

number of military development plans that had been ditched by his predecessor President Carter. Soon after his appointment as the new U.S. Defence Secretary, Caspar Weinberger announced that America was considering basing the neutron bomb in Europe. He thought this would enhance the possibility of N.A.T.O. being able to fight a 'limited' nuclear war in Europe. When this plan was originally mooted in 1977 it had to be abandoned because of fierce popular opposition in Europe and in Britain.

As the neutron bomb is rather different from the weapons already mentioned it will be useful to spend a moment describing it. The essential feature of this bomb is that the explosive power is greatly reduced while retaining the familiar radiation yield. In other words, it is a weapon capable of killing large numbers of people whilst leaving buildings intact (presumably so that the attacker could, after a few weeks' delay to allow radio-activity to die down, march in and possess the buildings).

All kinds of safeguards have been built into the defence systems of the nuclear powers to prevent the accidental use of strategic nuclear weapons. The late Professor Eric Burhop issued the following grave warning about the smaller weapons, particularly the neutron bomb:

'By contrast the so-called "tactical" weapons of which the neutron bomb is the latest, are built to be deployed in large numbers on the battlefield under the control of the commander on the spot, to be used in certain tactical situations. It is as certain as night follows day that their initial use would be followed by the use of larger nuclear weapons by the other side, leading to an escalation which there is nothing to stop short of the use of the largest available strategic nuclear weapons. Mankind and its whole future may be placed in jeopardy by the quick, trigger-happy decision of some field officer acting in emergency under conditions of great stress when cool judgement is impossible. This is perhaps the main threat posed by the neutron bomb and is indeed the Achilles heel of the whole N.A.T.O. military doctrine of first use of "tactical" nuclear weapons.'[18]

The position of Great Britain

During the 1950s and early 1960s Britain maintained an independent nuclear force of medium range bombers. By 1967 the first of Britain's Polaris submarines was in service. These carry strategic missiles. There are now four such submarines, each with 16 missiles fitted with three 200 kiloton warheads. These warheads are being replaced by the new Chevaline types developed at Aldermaston at a cost of £1,000 million. There are also the nuclear installations in the U.K. under the control of the U.S.A. and of N.A.T.O.

In 1980 the Conservative government announced its intention of replacing the Polaris fleet with Trident submarines at a cost of £5,000 million. These would come into service around the year 1990. The following through of this programme would mean a tremendous increase in Britain's nuclear fire power – from around 200 warheads to nearer 2,000.

The Royal Air Force has over 200 nuclear-capable aircraft. Naval helicopters can carry nuclear depth bombs to destroy submarines. The British Army of the Rhine is equipped with artillery missiles which can deliver warheads in the kiloton range.

In laying out all this statistical information it is easy enough to overlook the human element in the management of the military machine. Dr. Lawrence Freedman, who is Head of Policy Studies at the Royal Institute of International Affairs, deals with some aspects of this important side of the subject in a passage which is worth quoting in full:

'To reduce the vulnerability to Soviet anti-submarine measures the Polaris boats exploit their mobility moving from the safe, deep waters around Scotland to the vast expanses of the Atlantic Ocean. The length of each patrol is irregular, although around 10–12 weeks. Only a few know the route of the patrol. The boat will leave port in such a way as to confuse any waiting Soviet submarines wishing to trail it. At sea everything is done to avoid being noticed: the boat never surfaces and noise is kept down to a minimum; there is a doctor on board capable of performing emergency operations to avoid having to interrupt a patrol for medical reasons; radio silence is maintained so that there can be communications sent to the boat, but it sends no messages in return. The crew are positively vetted when they volunteer for Polaris duty. On patrol there has been far less homosexuality, mental illness, drug-taking or tormented consciences than originally expected.

'During patrol a constant watch is kept for signs of Soviet submarines. N.A.T.O. submarines, at least for the moment, are able to detect their Soviet counterparts before they are detected themselves. This allows time for evasive action. In wartime, if evasion was for some reason not possible, the Polaris boats could protect themselves against attack using their own torpedoes.

'A decision to launch the Polaris missiles could only be taken by the Prime Minister. However, Mrs. Thatcher could not initiate the launching procedure by herself. This would require the participation of at least one member of the Chiefs of Staff. A civil servant and military officer, with access to the relevant safes and codes, are always on hand. The captain of the submarine would be alerted by headquarters in London; in 15 minutes its missile could be ready for action. On the boat no single individual has all the information relevant to a missile launch, and the critical launch procedures have to be conducted by two senior officers. While the countdown is under way, the captain must keep a key inserted in a box. He can stop the countdown at any stage by removing it. These two officers are capable of launching the missiles of their own volition. The only circumstances in which they are permitted to even consider this are when they have reason to believe that Britain has been devastated by a nuclear attack and no responsible person is in a position to transmit orders to them. They must monitor all possible forms of communication (and there are many) before making any decision. To quote one Polaris commander: "You don't unleash Armageddon on the basis of radio silence!"

'Each boat carries hundreds of target tapes. The choice between them is made in London, although the captain has his own list in case a missile aborts and another has to be re-targeted to take its place. Once the firing begins there need only be 14 seconds between volleys; even less if the captain is prepared to take some risks with the boat's stability as water rushes in to fill the spaces vacated by the missiles. Once all the missiles are released, the submarine changes mission and prepares to make use of the torpedoes it also carries on board in attacks on the enemy navy. By this time the crew could only assume that little would be left of its own country.'[19]

Dr. Freedman's book is a detailed description of the evolution of Britain's policy on nuclear weapons and concludes with a cool assessment of the strategic and political arguments for and against our remaining a nuclear power.

Ever since the 1950s Britain has talked in terms of her 'contribution to N.A.T.O.'s nuclear deterrent', but Dr. Freedman suggests that there is need for more questioning both of the idea of independence and of deterrent effect in the phrase 'the independent nuclear deterrent' which is used in this connection.

Part of the argument in favour of Britain's independent nuclear deterrent is that it gives N.A.T.O. a separate centre of decision-making in Europe (as distinct from decisions made by the U.S.A.), and thus increases the sense of uncertainty in a possible agressor. This seems a very flimsy argument; it sounds just as reasonable to suggest that such uncertainty detracts from deterrence by raising doubts about the quality and resolution of the decisions of the alliance as a whole. In any case it is extraordinarily difficult to imagine any scenario in which Britain would decide unilaterally to use her nuclear weapons. To do so would provoke an immediate response involving total devastation of the United Kingdom. From the strictly military point of view it is likely to be increasingly difficult to maintain the argument for Britain's retaining nuclear weapons. The crippling cost of doing so, which is always increasing, and the consequent declining contribution to conventional forces, only increases reliance on nuclear weapons with the attendant dangers.

Another argument advanced by those who favour retention by Britain of its nuclear weapons is that this ensures her a prominent position in international affairs and a significant 'voice at the conference table'. It is, however, an inescapable fact that Britain's influence in the world of power politics has continued steadily to decline during all the years that she has been a nuclear power. Many people, including politicians, seem still to be living in the past and suffering from delusions of imperial grandeur. It surely is a sign of maturity to face the facts of life and recognize Britain's changed position in the world. Only so can we be saved from the reckless diversion of our resources away from the real needs of the country into expensive projects which are irrelevant to our situation.

This chapter has been mainly concerned to present a number of facts and some opinions. We have not yet entered upon the detailed moral debate which the facts provoke. It is neither possible nor desirable to separate the moral and political aspects of the discussion, but it is of interest to note that many of the political pointers are in the direction of Britain's adopting a more neutralist foreign policy.

Conventional weapons

Another comment must be made before we proceed to the next stage of our enquiry. This book deals mainly with the nuclear question, and with the most horrific developments in the field of warfare. It must not be assumed, however, that this indicates any lack of concern about so-called 'conventional' weapons. Many millions of people have been killed in armed conflicts since the end of the Second World War, and this without the use of any nuclear weapons. We must not forget, either, the existence of chemical and biological methods of warfare. Vast devastation was caused in Indo-china by the use of chemicals. The U.S.A. destroyed huge areas of forest and crops in South Vietnam by spraying them with herbicides. It is estimated that enough food was destroyed to feed 900,000 people for a year.

It might have been supposed that the development of nuclear weapons would have led to a lessening of the impetus to produce new and more lethal conventional weapons, but this has not happened. The continued production of these lesser but increasingly horrendous instruments of death imposes enormous economic strains on both developed and developing countries. It is in fact conventional armaments that have contributed most to the militarization of our societies.

Apart from the destruction of life and property in war, though related to it, there is the human cost as described by Alva Myrdal:

'There are more subtle effects, even without actual war,

when masses of men are held in occupation armies and military bases. These are social costs which make for long-term distortion of normalcy: the moral degradation of soldiers who become accustomed in their young and formative years to drugs, brothels, black markets – and, of course, to brutality. In the spate of self-incriminating comments after the end of the United States' active involvement in the Indochinese war, many sombre facts were being reported about the 2.5 million American veterans who served in Southeast Asia:

'Of those who were married before they went to Vietnam, 38 per cent were separated or getting divorced six months after their return.

'As many as 175,000 probably have used heroin since getting out of service.

'Over 400,000 servicemen who had participated in fighting were given other than honorable discharges.

'For the young Vietnam-era veteran, the ex-soldier of age twenty to twenty-four, unemployed rates have been running above 18 per cent. If one looks at the black veterans' sub-group within this category (twenty to twenty-four years of age) the rates approximate 30 per cent.

'Of the 124,000 draft evaders and deserters eligible for clemency, only some 20,000 ever applied.

'One hears of and cares about the hundreds of thousands of children fathered by American soldiers and left in Vietnam. Why is nothing said about the moral conditions of the men who abandoned them? Or about the guilt of soldiers, from generals to GIs, who turned hundreds of thousands of Indochinese women into prostitutes? Men engaged in the time-honored male pursuit of warfare are evidently supposed to have the right to enjoy themselves – at the cost of women and children. Effects such as these are usually not counted as costs of war. But they should be.'[20]

Any programme of disarmament must seek reduction and eventual abolition of all arms.

How are we to assess the attempts that have been made to begin to disarm a world which has been so fearfully disfigured by the mildew of militarism? To that question we must now turn our attention.

4: Cobwebs spun across the cannon's mouth

The time is short. I believe that only a bold step can save civilization. If Mankind continues to make atomic bombs without changing the political relationship between states, sooner or later these bombs will be used for mutual annihilation.

Clement Attlee in a letter to
President Truman.

Naught for your comfort

For the Christian despair is not an option. He has a duty to be hopeful and can only discharge that duty because hope is a gift of God. It is just as well, because few things are more calculated, from every human point of view, to induce despair than a survey of the attempts made in recent years to achieve some real progress towards disarmament. Christian hopefulness is not a superficial optimism derived from a resolute refusal to look facts in the face. Rather it is a quality of resilience that even in the face of clearly-recognized and mountainous difficulties refuses to give up the struggle.

From the figures already quoted in this book it is clear that, far from disarming, the nations of the world have for the most part been spending more and more on the machinery of death. It might therefore be assumed that no real attempts have been made to grapple with the problem. That would be very far from the truth. In fact disarmament talks might be described as a flourishing even if largely unproductive industry. It employs large numbers of people in well-paid posts. But what has been achieved? Elizabeth Young asserts: 'It would not be unfair to say that during the sixties the superpowers have colluded in presenting to the world a series of insignificant treaties at very considerable expense of international time and trouble and breath'.[21] They have been little more than 'a cobweb spun across the mouth of the cannon'.[22]

For an exhaustive account of more than a quarter of a century's disarmament discussions we have to turn to another woman writer. Mrs. Alva Myrdal, as Sweden's former Minister of Disarmament, was over many years at the centre of the struggles to achieve some measure of progress in reversing the arms race which she describes as 'a global folly'. Her treatment of the subject is of particular value, not only because of her detailed knowledge and first-hand experience, but also because she was involved as the representative of a neutral country. Sweden some years ago formally and un-ilaterally renounced nuclear weapons and all chemical and biological means of warfare. It is refreshing to look at the issues confronting us not through the eyes of those who are, or imagine themselves to be, representatives of great powers, but rather from the point of view – manifestly less partial – of a representative of a non-aligned state.

Alva Myrdal's judgement is a sobering one and echoes that of Elizabeth Young. The story thus far is 'a history of lost opportunities'. The 1970s were named by the Secretary-General of the U.N. as 'a Disarmament Decade', but Mrs. Myrdal sums up:

'Let me immediately reveal how the experiences of a decade of disarmament efforts have gradually led me and many others participating in these efforts to some terrifying conclusions: that we have accomplished no real disarma-ment, that we can see hardly any tangible results of our work, and that the underlying major cause must be that the super-powers have not seriously tried to achieve disarmament.

'Those who have power have no will to disarm. At least they constantly demonstrate this by negative response to each and all of the proposals that would entail genuine arms limitation.

'The history of disarmament should have been a series of positive, purposeful, effective steps towards the goal which is acclaimed by everybody. We are still waiting for a first decisive, or even a serious, step to be taken.'[23]

Why is it that so little progress has been made and what has actually been happening on the disarmament front over these past years?

The reasons for our failure

The major blame for the continued escalation of the arms race must be laid at the door of the two super-powers, Russia and the U.S.A. It is they who have determined the scale and the pace of rearmament and dragged much of the rest of the world along in the wake of their insane policies. In the period immediately following the second world war the attitude towards Russia inside Europe was markedly different from that adopted by the U.S.A. Although there was disapproval by European countries of Soviet annexation of the Baltic States there was a measure of understanding of Russia's desire to establish a belt of buffer states against Germany, at whose hands she had suffered so much. But the Americans took a different view. Anti-Communist sentiment increased and the cold war began. The massive build-up of arms began, led by the two super-powers but engulfing more and more nations.

Once a country becomes enmeshed in the business of rearming all kinds of forces combine to make it difficult to reverse the process. More and more people come to depend for their livelihood on employment in the arms industry. The power of what President Eisenhower called the 'military-industrial complex' expands. Increasing amounts of money are spent on military research and development: very many times more than is spent on health research. Many highly lucrative posts are available to scientists in the field of military research. They find themselves caught up in a self-generating process in which the goal is always new and more sophisticated devices. Questions about the need for such devices and considerations of ultimate aims are squeezed out of consciousness by the relentless pressure of the demand for 'progress'.

The arms race is the product of fear and mistrust but it also helps to create a deepening of these corrosive attitudes: it is a vicious circle. If Russia is afraid of the U.S.A. there need be no mystery about the reason. American missiles are targeted on Russian cities and there is increasing talk of a willingness to deploy those weapons in a 'pre-emptive first strike' – euphemism for obliterating millions of Russian citizens. Russia has every reason to feel vulnerable. She has an immense land boundary to defend and in two world wars suffered devastation of her cities with millions of dead and an economy gravely disrupted. But equally America fears Russia and for similar though not identical reasons. The U.S.A. contributed decisively to the winning of both world wars but each time emerged with her homeland intact and actually richer than when she entered the wars. But Americans know it would not be the same next time, and that weapons of inconceivable destructive power are trained on their cities by a country which has embraced an alien creed and is constantly presented as power-hungry with dreams of global hegemony.

These, then, are some of the reasons for the virtual stalemate in the efforts thus far to achieve a real and significant measure of disarmament. It is against that background that we must look at some of the details of the search for agreement over the past twenty or so years.

Is there any point in treaties?

It is often alleged in popular debate that all the time-consuming efforts to draft international treaties and solemnly to sign and then ratify them is a waste of time. The implication is that a state will only abide by the terms of a treaty so long as it believes that its own interests are thereby served, but will unhesitatingly break them if it believes otherwise. Usually, of course, those who so argue think of other nations breaking their treaty obligations and not their own.

Those who argue in this way may be surprised to read the quite different judgement of some of those experts in international law who have made a detailed study of the subject. So Louis Henkin asserts:

'The law works all the time. With few, isolated, sporadic exceptions, nations daily live up to the obligations of thousands of treaties, to the responsibilities and duties of states under customary law, even when there might be substantial interest and substantial temptation to violate law or when, if there were no law, nations would freely act otherwise'.[24]

In many ways international law is different from the ordinary law of the land as the citizens of all countries know it. The observance of rules is part of the life-style of government bureaucrats of every sort and they do not easily accept the idea of breaking them. Furthermore, whereas the law of the land is something imposed upon ordinary citizens – though for the most part willingly accepted by the great majority of them – international law is the result of agreement *between* states. Having freely accepted the terms of a treaty they are most likely thereafter to comply with them.

Nicholas A. Sims states that treaties have a number of 'social functions'. He refers to seven of these which may be summarized as follows:

'First, a treaty reinforces existing restraints on behaviour by adding legal reasons to the inhibitions deriving from moral and prudential motives.

'Second, a treaty (if well drafted) clarifies the state of the law on any subject.

'Third, as a result of this formalisation, the likelihood of adverse publicity becomes a more potent restraint on a subsequent change of mind by governments.

'Fourth, a treaty, if it gains widespread acceptance, sets a standard of internationally acceptable behaviour which other states, even though they are not parties to the treaty, must at least take into account in making policy.

'Fifth, the existence of a treaty *may* provide evidence in the future of the evolution of a general rule of international law, more universally binding on states than the treaty itself.

'Sixth, a treaty may bring into existence a new international organisation, or strengthen an existing one, in such a way as to strengthen the hand of those who have an interest in ensuring that states comply with their international obligations.

'Last, but not least, a treaty may have a useful effect in conditioning public and diplomatic opinion to an expectation of further treaties, making the negotiation of agreements appear a normal activity of international life.'[25]

Multilateral efforts towards arms control

Disarmament is discussed every year in the regular sessions of the U.N. General Assembly and from time to time, as in 1978, in special sessions. There is also a U.N. Disarmament

Commission to which all U.N. members belong. In 1962 a body known as the Eighteen-Nation Disarmament Committee was set up by the U.N. General Assembly. This was later expanded and is now referred to as the Geneva Committee on Disarmament. There are a great many other bodies, some bilateral and some multilateral, concerned with detailed questions of regional arms control, categories of weapons and technical problems.

We now briefly examine some of the major efforts that have been made to control the production and use of arms.

1. *The Baruch Plan.*

This was put forward by the U.S.A. in 1946 and was aimed at placing all nuclear operations which threatened world security under international ownership and control. At this crucial point in history a great opportunity was lost. The Baruch Plan contained a number of sensible proposals but it was basically unfair in that it assigned somewhat vague obligations to the Americans whilst imposing on the Soviet Union obligations that were strict and, by comparison, harsh. The Soviet delegate to the U.N. Security Council put forward a counter-proposal to destroy all nuclear weapons already in existence and forthwith to cease production. These proposals were completely unacceptable to the Americans who were unwilling to sacrifice the advantage which they imagine belonged to them as the first in the field. They immediately proceeded to conduct the first of their post-war atomic tests over Bikini on the 1st July, 1946. The failure of the Baruch Plan is an indication of the dismal pattern of subsequent negotiations by the super-powers. All too often both sides have presented proposals including conditions which it was quite clear the other side would be unwilling to accept.

2. *The Partial Test Ban Treaty.*

This was signed in Moscow on the 5th August, 1963. It had been negotiated by the U.S.A., the U.S.S.R. and Britain. It banned all nuclear explosions which would release radioactivity on an international scale. By the end of 1977 this treaty had been accepted by 108 States. France and China, however, did not accept it and between them conducted some 60 atmospheric tests between 1963 and 1977. France agreed to discontinue her tests in the atmosphere in 1965, when she felt that militarily she had caught up on the first three nuclear powers and could now, like them, transfer the testing underground.

Some have criticised the Partial Test Ban Treaty as being little more than a "clean air bill". It is true that it has little to do with disarmament as such, but it has some value particularly in demonstrating the possibility of firm agreements between the super-powers, and also in preventing the pollution of the atmosphere caused by tests above ground.

3. Treaties relating to uninhabited territories

A devout steward in the vestry prayed the following prayer before an evening church service: 'O Lord, bless all the people who live in the uninhabited lands'. Not surprisingly, agreement has been most easily secured with reference to areas devoid of inhabitants and without boundaries or governments. There are three treaties to which reference must be made.

a) The Antarctic Treaty 1959

This was negotiated by 19 States that have a particular interest in the area, and it bans all military manoeuvres, bases and nuclear testing.

b) The Peaceful Uses of Outer Space Treaty 1967

By the end of 1977 some 77 States had accepted the terms of this treaty. It bans all military maneouvres, bases and testing on 'celestial bodies'. In 1971 Russia put forward a proposal that the provisions of this treaty should be re-enacted with regard to the moon; (in view of man's first steps in the conquest of space a not unreasonable suggestion). It was referred to the U.N. Committee on the peaceful uses of outer space, but no action has, as yet, been taken.

c) The Sea Bed Treaty 1971

Something like 70% of the surface of the globe is covered by the sea. This treaty seeks to exclude this vast area from the nuclear arms race. Many believe that the amount of time and trouble taken in negotiating the treaty is in no way commensurate with the meagre benefits resulting from it. By the end of 1977, 65 States had signified their agreement to the treaty.

Perhaps one significant virtue of these three treaties concerned with various aspects of the environment is that they give evidence of a concern by the international community to preserve the idea of a 'common heritage' of mankind.

4. *Other treaties*

a) *The Convention on Environmental Modification 1977.*

This arose out of an initiative taken by the Soviet Union. The Convention bans the use for military purposes of any environmental techniques which have 'widespread, long-lasting or severe effects'. The terms of this convention may sound rather far-fetched, but remind us of the extraordinary developments in the world of applied science. The techniques referred to are those that may affect weather patterns, the generation of tidal waves and the melting of ice-caps. In Laos America endeavoured to precipitate rainfall for military purposes by pelting clouds with a silver iodied aerosol. Other techniques having a variety of deleterious effects on the living environment are already part of the history of modern warfare.

b) *Treaty of Tlatelolco 1967*

The importance of this treaty is that it represents the first successful attempt to create a nuclear weapon free zone in an inhabited area. The treaty is now in force among 22 of the 24 States in Latin America which have ratified it. It bans the testing, use, manufacture, production or acquisition of any nuclear weapons by the States which adhere to it. Whilst it may be thought that it is unlikely that any of the Latin American States may want or be able to acquire nuclear weapons, this treaty must be regarded as of exemplary value, and credit is due to the Latin American members of the U.N. whose initiative led to the drafting of the treaty.

c) *The Convention on Biological and Toxin Weapons 1972*

This convention prohibits the development, production and stockpiling of biological and toxin weapons. It also provides for the destruction of existing stocks. It could be said that this is the first international treaty which actually provides for a real measure of disarmament. It is true that America – the only country in the world to admit in recent years to possessing biological weapons – unilaterally renounced those weapons in 1969, but there may be other countries that have had stocks of biological weapons. 76 States had ratified the terms of the convention by the end of 1977. It is to be hoped that this treaty will enable progress to be made in the related matter of the abandonment of chemical weapons.

d) *The Non-proliferation Treaty 1968*

At first sight it might seem to be an eminently wise and sensible suggestion to establish a non-proliferation treaty. In fact, however, the negotiations which led to this particular treaty were prolonged and bitter. Altogether they extended over five years from 1965 to 1970 and during that period held the centre of the disarmament stage. In fact, however, the treaty did not lead to any measure of disarmament whatsoever.

Those who promoted the non-proliferation treaty aimed to stop the spread of nuclear weapons to any countries other than the five which already possess them. The non-nuclear weapon states from the beginning saw the treaty as grossly discriminatory. They were being asked to eschew what obviously the five nuclear states saw as the great military advantage of possessing the most powerful weapons ever produced. The nuclear states were being asked to do nothing in return. The response of the nuclear weapon states to this was to point to the fact that nuclear weapons were immensely costly to produce and dangerous to handle. The treaty could have been of great value if it had been used as a lever to secure a real measure of disarmament: in fact, it proved to be no more than a consolidation of the nuclear status quo. As noted on p. 56, a considerable number of militarily significant countries have not signed the treaty.

Even the most favourable assessment of the efforts briefly reviewed above must conclude that they have resulted not so much in progress towards disarmament as in the institutionalization of the continuing arms race. Nicholas Sims gives his own careful judgement of the strictly limited value of what has been achieved:

'We need not write off the diplomacy of arms limitation as cosmetic, collusive or insignificant. Parts of it have deserved all those epithets. Other parts have not. There is enough of lasting value in the latter for those who pursue the more ambitious goal of disarmament to feel some gratitude towards those who made the better treaties possible, even though they have not taken us far towards disarmament. For what evidence is there that these treaties actually distracted the world from negotiating general and complete disarmament? Is it not just as likely that in their absence we would have got, not GCD, but nothing at all?'[26]

Bilateral talks

The strategic arms limitation talks (SALT) differ from those which led to the treaties already mentioned in that they were conducted exclusively by the two super-powers, the U.S.A. and the U.S.S.R. The SALT negotiations have concentrated on the so-called strategic weapons systems, that is those that are designed to serve direct hits on each other's homelands. The first SALT agreements were signed at a summit ceremony in Moscow during the visit of President Richard Nixon to the then General Secretary of the Soviet Communist Party, Leonid Brezhnev. Those agreements covered a variety of issues two of which referred specifically to arms limitation. They were headed: 'A Treaty between the United States of America and the Union of Soviet Socialist Republics on the limitation of anti-ballistic missile systems' and 'Interim Agreement between the United States of America and the Union of Soviet Socialist Republics on certain measures with respect to the limitation of strategic offensive arms'. Alas, these agreements had nothing whatever to do with disarmament. They represent a haggling about agreed numbers and, in fact, the ceilings discussed were so high as not to involve any sacrifice of weapon development on either side. Indeed, it is not unfair to say that the SALT agreements are about the continuation of the arms race to an agreed and higher level. The nuclear arms race has in fact now moved from a race for quantity to a race for quality, but the SALT agreements include no prohibition on qualitative improvements in weaponry. From one point of view the SALT agreements can only mean that the super-powers are more shackled in respect of any real attempts to move towards a de-escalation of the arms race. The agreements virtually recognise the rightness of the two super-powers continuing to match each other's ever-increasing military might. One of the few gleams of light is the fact that both sides seem to have been more willing than hitherto to declare the actual numbers of the strategic weapons they possess. SALT I, however, does not deal with the enormous numbers of tactical nuclear weapons deployed by both sides.

Further discussions are taking place on a second round of agreements (SALT II). Progress, if any, is extremely slow and it remains to be seen whether these latest talks are likely to be more successful than the earlier ones.

The hollow absurdity of the situation in which the nuclear powers have become enmeshed is brought out in a telling quotation from Herbert York who was Director of Defense Research and Engineering in the Department of Defense under Presidents Eisenhower and Kennedy:

'If one, or ten, or maybe a few hundred bombs on target are all that are needed to deter, how did it happen that we came to possess more than 10,000? And why so much total explosive power? These numbers are *not* the result of a careful calculation of the need in some specific strategic or tactical situation. They are the result of a series of historical accidents which have been rationalized after the fact. In the late 1940s and early 1950s, before the invention of the H-bomb, it was determined that we needed on the order of 1,000 delivery vehicles (then land-based and sea-based bombers) in our strategic forces . . . Then suddenly, when the H-bomb was perfected in 1954, the explosive power of the bombs multiplied 1,000-fold. When the effectiveness of each nuclear weapon was thus so enormously increased, one might have supposed it would have resulted in a reduction in the number of delivery vehicles needed, *but no such adjustment was made*. In fact, because the perfection of the H-bomb was one of the technological advances that made long-range missiles practical, the H-bomb actually resulted in a proliferation of types of delivery systems. . . . In the late 1960s, further technolgical advances made it possible to provide each individual missile with more than ten individually-targetable warheads.

Again, one might have expected some adjustment in the number of delivery vehicles, but there was none . . . In brief then, even if we accept for the time being the need for a policy of deterrence through mutual assured destruction, the forces now in being are enormously greater than are needed for that purpose.'[27]

The way ahead

At the end of a lengthy and detailed review of disarmament negotiations to which several references have already been made, Alva Myrdal sets out the case for the calling of a World Disarmament Conference. She is, however, quite clear that if such a conference is to meet with any success it requires as a pre-condition the making of two principal security guarantees. The first of these is a pledge on the part of the nuclear powers not to initiate any act of nuclear warfare. The second is a pledge not to attack any nuclear-weapons-free country with nuclear weapons. China has laid it down as a pre-condition for its participation in a world disarmament conference that guarantees should be made in advance. Many non-aligned countries have made the same plea. On the assumption that these two pledges were forthcoming Mrs. Mrydal proceeds to outline some of the major questions that such a world disarmament conference should discuss. These include: quantitative disarmament of nuclear weapons and their delivery vehicles; qualitative disarmament of nuclear weapons; similar quantitative as well as qualitative disarmament of conventional weapons; prohibition of production, stockpiling, trading and deployment of chemical weapons; prohibition of the use, as well as the production of cruel anti-personnel weapons; prohibition of indiscriminate warfare befalling civilian populations, as well as prohibition of environmental warfare; agreements on the demilitarisation of ocean space; and agreements on eliminating foreign bases.

Even if the prospect of such a multilateral world conference does not look particularly bright at the present time, there are initiatives that the non-nuclear and non-aligned states could take. Arms limitation agreements can be reached independently of the super-powers. The decision to establish an international verification agency could be made in the

United Nations by a majority vote. It would be possible for a disarmament conference of non-nuclear weapons states to be held. Such a conference which would, of course, mean very careful and adequate preparation could sharpen the demands that are being made all over the world for nuclear disarmament, and could establish an agenda for continuing and realistic independent action by the non-nuclear weapons states in relation to a whole number of disarmament issues.

What has been said in this chapter about the activities of politicians and negotiators in the disarmament field must surely be sufficient to erode any comfortable belief on the part of ordinary people like ourselves that we can safely 'leave it all to the experts'. There is at the present time not only much evidence of a ground-swell of popular public concern about disarmament all over the world, but also an indication that the pressures of public opinion can affect in vital ways the course of political debate and decision. The implications of that fact will engage our minds again when we come to the final chapter.

One of the reasons for the widespread dissatisfaction with the ineffectiveness of the attempts to slow down and reverse the arms race is the realization that continuing failure inhibits all the efforts to deal with the problems of poverty, hunger and disease. The piling up of munitions means in effect that millions of people, especially children, are killed without a shot being fired. They die because money that should be spent on relief and development is squandered on arms. It is to this aspect of our subject that we now turn.

5: The struggle for survival

The task is to free mankind from dependence and oppression, from hunger and distress. New links must be developed which substantially increase the chances of achieving freedom, justice and solidarity for all. This is a great task for both the present generation and for the next.

Herr Willy Brandt

'Whom the Gods destroy . . .'

In despite of the prophet's words,
We beat our plough-shares into swords,
    Our pruning-hooks to spears.
We forge horrendous tools for war,
Blindly the lessons we ignore,
    Spelt out by blood-drenched years.

Bemused by make-belief and lies,
We perpetrate in modern guise
    Ancient barbarities;
Whole generations yet unborn,
Inheritors of woe, may mourn
    Our inhumanities.

On homes and schools we must spend less;
On welfare, health, and happiness
    We must economise;
Yet Trident and its grisly train
Dread instruments of grief and pain,
    We think essential buys.

Blandly we call for strife to cease.
We bid small nations live in peace,

A happy brotherhood.
Then we compete to sell them arms,
Vile trade, inflicting deadly harms,
   The price is paid in blood.

Hungry, the world's poor children cry,
In tragic millions doomed to die,
   We care not why or how;
While wealth beyond all bounds is spent
On vast destructive armament –
   Where is compassion now?

Stanley Finch,
July 1981

Christians awake

This poem arrived on my desk as I was about to begin the writing of this chapter. It came from a fellow Methodist minister and expresses the agony of mind and conscience felt by increasing numbers of people, Christians and others, at the appalling contradictions which face us in a world deeply divided between rich and poor, and in which the prodigal squandering of precious resources on military equipment and programmes robs us of vital munitions needed for the war on want.

No other issue has taken deeper root in the conscience of Christians in recent years than this concern for the under-privileged. It finds expression in all kinds of ways. There is increasing emphasis on the importance of simpler life-styles – 'Live simply that others may simply live'. The relief and development agencies of the Churches have drawn Christians together in common ecumenical enterprizes. This is not only good in itself but represents an educational exercise of the greatest importance.

The concern of the Churches is not, however, just for the amelioration of the lot of the poor. The dispensing of charity has always been a charge on Christian generosity, but something more than that is needed if our response to the imperatives of the gospel is to be more adequate. Dr. Philip Potter states the issue with characteristic clarity:

'Our experience has taught us that this matter needs to be approached at a deeper and more fundamental level. Development efforts so far have been powerless to redress the gap between the rich and the poor between and within nations. On the contrary, the gap grows wider every year. The world food crisis is only one tragic consequence of the widening gap. Several years of involvement in development aid have convinced us that a purely economic growth concept working automatically for development should be replaced by a process aimed at economic and social justice, self-reliance, and people's participation in establishing goals and priorities and making decisions regarding economic growth as a means to the end of a globally just society.'[28]

As they have wrestled with the problems of poverty, hunger and disease, the Churches have more and more recognized that they are involved in the search for justice. This is reflected not only in the setting up of Church-related bodies with titles like 'The Commission on Justice and Peace', but also in the liturgies which are at the heart of Christian worship. Opening the Methodist Service Book almost at random I read the following bidding:

'I ask your prayers for the peace of the world,
for the rulers of all nations,
for government in accordance with God's holy will,
and for a just and proper use of the natural resources
of the world.'

Concern for justice is a theme to which many preachers frequently turn, drawing inspiration from passages like the one in the Prophet Amos which reflects the displeasure of the Almighty at religious ceremonial unrelated to the real needs of His world:

'I hate, I spurn your pilgrim-feasts;
I will not delight in your sacred ceremonies. When you
    present your sacrifices and offerings I will not accept
them,
Nor look on the buffaloes of your shared-offerings.
Spare me the sound of your songs;
I cannot endure the music of your lutes.

Let justice roll on like a river
and righteousness like an ever-flowing stream.'

(Amos 5:21–24)

The great divide

One of the most widely-quoted documents of recent times is the Report of the Brandt Commission. This was produced by a remarkable group of international statesmen and leaders led by Willy Brandt of Germany. It is entitled 'North–South: A Programme for Survival'. The cover design is a reproduction of a map of the world divided across the middle by a thick black line. Whilst it is true that the South includes such rich countries as Australia and New Zealand, it is a rather startling fact that 'North' and 'South' are broadly synonymous with 'rich' and 'poor'. Here is how the Brandt Report sees this great divide:

'The nations of the South see themselves as sharing a common predicament. Their solidarity in global negotiations stems from the awareness of being dependent on the North, and unequal with it; and a great many of them are bound together by their colonial experience. The North including Eastern Europe has a quarter of the world's population and four-fifths of its income; the South including China has three billion people – three-quarters of the world's population but living on one-fifth of the world's income. In the North, the average person can expect to live for more than seventy years; he or she will rarely be hungry, and will be educated at least up to secondary level. In the countries of the South the great majority of people have a life expectancy of closer to fifty years; in the poorest countries one out of every four children dies before the age of five; one-fifth or more of all the people in the South suffer from hunger and malnutrition; fifty per cent have no chance to become literate.

'Behind these differences lies the fundamental inequality of economic strength. It is not just that the North is so much richer than the South. Over 90 per cent of the world's manufacturing industry is in the North. Most patents and new technology are the property of multinational corporations of the North, which conduct a large share of world investment and world trade in raw materials and manufactures. Because of this economic power northern countries dominate the international economic system – its rules and regulations, and its international institutions of trade, money and finance. Some developing countries have swum against this tide, taking the opportunities which exist and overcoming many obstacles; but most of them find the currents too strong for them. In the world as in nations, economic forces left entirely to themselves tend to produce growing inequality. Within nations public policy has to protect the weaker partners. The time has come to apply this precept to relations between nations within the world community.'[29]

It is inescapably true that there can be no peace in a world so deeply divided by glaring inequalities and injustices. Christian compassion and ordinary prudential considerations both point to the fact that the war on want must be prosecuted with urgency and resolution. Let us consider more closely some of the basic facts of life in a world where it is increasingly clear that the attempt to secure justice is quite literally a struggle for survival.

Noah's new flood

This century has witnessed what can only be described as a demographic deluge. Brief reference was made at the beginning of chapter 3 to 'Noah's new flood' – of people. Statistics are an inadequate guide to the magnitude of what has happened. In the nature of the case they cannot be strictly accurate, and, anyhow, our imaginations tend to shut off when we are faced with astronomical figures. Nevertheless since people matter it is important that we make an effort to grasp the significance of the statistics. It is human beings who make history, and that history will be shaped, among other things, by how many there are of us, where we live, and the patterns of our migrations.

There are interesting, not to say alarming, parallels between the growth of world population and the increase in man's destructive capacity. So far as the latter is concerned men advanced only very slowly at first from the use of slings and stones (such as David used to kill Goliath) to bows and arrows, swords and spears and similar weapons. With the invention of gunpowder a new era began: small guns were replaced by larger ones, little bombs by bigger ones, and in next to no time we had progressed, if indeed that word can be so demeaned, through saturation bombing to the obscenities of the age of overkill.

Now consider the way the size of the world's population has increased. Before the discovery of agriculture, about 6,000 B.C., the world's population was probably less than 20 millions (or twice the present population of Greater London). It did not pass the 100 millions until after the time of the Old Kingdom of Egypt. When Jesus was born it was probably about 150 millions. It took a further six centuries to double. By the year 1700 A.D. world population was 600 millions. But now watch the figures carefully. The next doubling took only 150 years and the next after that a bare 100 years. But after that the rate of acceleration reached explosive force: 2,500 millions had been reached by 1950 and this became 3,000 millions by 1960 and 4,000 millions by 1980. Nearly all the estimates made by the experts have turned out to be too low. When in 1949 the U.N. decided to convene a conference on population, by the time it met, five years later, the size of the global family had grown by 130 millions.

Many factors affect population trends. Each major advance in numbers has followed some new discovery or invention such as that of agricultural methods, the beginning of urban settlements and of trade, the harnessing of non-human energy, and the marvels of modern technology. The most recent factor decisively to affect population levels has been the application of scientific medicine. In fact death-control has advanced more rapidly than birth-control. In Sri Lanka, for example, malaria was virtually eradicated in five years, thanks to DDT and a well-organized campaign. As a consequence of this and other public health measures the death rate was reduced from 22 to 12 per thousand in seven years – a fall which took ten times as long in England.

It takes time for new ideas to permeate the human consciousness. In the developing countries generally the possession of a large family has traditionally been linked with the economic need to have plenty of children to work on the land. Since many children died in infancy the number of births must always exceed the number of children dictated by economic necessity. A very different situation emerges when children have to be expensively educated and when most of those born survive to become adults. Even so it takes time for men and women to adjust to the facts of life especially when deep religious feelings are involved. In 1965 when Senator Robert F. Kennedy was visiting Peru he shouted to an exuberant crowd (referring to his own nine children): 'I challenge any of you to produce more children than I have'. That raised a cheer in Catholic Latin America but in many other parts of the world the response would have been a frown of disapproval.

The impact of rapid population increase on a nation and its future prospects was brought home to me very vividly on a recent visit to Zimbabwe. The African majority in that young state numbers about 6½ million. The rate of growth among them is 3.6 per cent per annum. That means more than 600 new mouths to feed every day. It also means that about half the African population are under fifteen years of age. The problem of finding work for such vast numbers is a daunting one. The prospect of soaring unemployment and the discontent that it breeds is frightening.

Population growth appears to pass through various stages. In the first stage both the birthrate and the deathrate are high; the result of that equation is that population increases, but slowly. In the next stage the death rate falls steeply but the birthrate remains high; as a consequence the population grows rapidly. In the third phase the birthrate comes down and so the rate of population increase is slowed. Finally birthrate and deathrate stabilise at a low level, after which the population tends to grow only very slowly.

The science of demography is still comparatively young. Its originator was an amiable Anglican priest called Thomas Malthus who, in 1798, published his 'Essay on the Principle of Population'. His thesis was that population tends, unless checked, to grow more rapidly than resources. The number of mouths to be fed will, he argues, always outstrip the capacity to supply their needs. The checks on population growth may be the result of evil things like disease and war. One obvious cure for hunger is to kill off the hungry. Malthus, of course, emphasizes the importance of those moral restraints like delayed marriage, premarital continence, and 'subjection of the passions to the guidance of reason'.

The thesis set out by Malthus has been attacked from many different points of view and few, if any, would wish today to defend it in detail. The demographic debate is highly complex and, as in most other fields, the experts do not always agree. To take but one example, nearly thirty years ago a fascinating book was written by Josué de Castro entitled 'Geography of Hunger'. The crucial point of his argument was 'that overpopulation does not cause starvation in various parts of the world, but that starvation is the cause of overpopulation'.[30] The reason for this paradoxical judgement is the alleged fact that hunger increases the fertility of depressed people. It is nature's way of compensating for excessive mortality: fertile indeed is the bed of misery. Part of the Malthusian theory is thereby stood on its head. Far from being a natural check on population growth, hunger is seen as a factor which promotes it; whereas adequate feeding and higher standards of living generally act as a brake on human fecundity. The argument is strengthened by the recognition that those who are rendered weak and ailing by hunger and sickness cannot, even if they have a job, put in a good day's work and so renew the stocks on the pantry shelves. They consume but they do not produce. Healthy well-fed citizens, however, can make an adequate contribution to their own sustenance.

A modern approach to the problem of population explosion stresses the need for attack on every front. Improving the standards of living of the underprivileged is one essential way of bringing the problem under control, and that means a multi-faceted approach. Equally, education in methods of family limitation is urgently needed. That is not just a matter of teaching techniques, but also of breaking down cultural and psychological inhibitions which hinder the acceptance of the whole idea of planned parenthood. The search for contraceptive devices which are simple, reliable and cheap is an important adjunct to the global programme of education now being conducted by a great variety of agents.

There are many, including some Roman Catholics, who deeply regret the continued insistence of the Roman Catholic Church that the use of 'artificial' contraceptives to plan and space children in marriage is sinful. That view is stated clearly by Father Robert I. Gannon:

'It (the Church) has to keep on condemning contraception, not because some Pope or Council forbade it, but because she still sees it as a violation of the Natural Law, as a perversion of right order which destroys the meaningfulness of the marriage act and creates as many difficulties as it seeks to avoid, whether moral, physical, psychological, or merely aesthetic.'[31]

The trouble with that judgement, quite apart from what many would regard as its defective basis in philosophy and theology, is that it really does not square with the facts of life as many devout Christian married couples experience them. While it is true that the Roman Catholic Church shares with others a deep concern about the population problem and approves the use of the 'rhythm method' to control conception, it is very much to be hoped that it will abandon a restrictive view which many regard as unrealistic and wrong.

It is certainly not part of the argument in this section that there is anything wrong *per se* in the increase in our numbers. In the very first chapter of the Bible God says to Adam and Eve: 'Be fruitful and increase, fill the earth and subdue it' (Genesis 1:28). But Jesus said: 'I have come that men may have life, and may have it in all its fullness' (John 10:10). This is part of God's new commandment and it has quantitative as well as qualitative relevance.

In the context of this book we must pay particular attention to the connection between population pressures and war. A good deal of nonsense has been written about this, suggesting that hunger and malnutrition are the direct causes of aggression. On the whole this is a false view. Major wars have usually been started by comparatively wealthy countries. Germany, Italy and Japan were in the 'have' category compared with the 'have-nots' whom they attacked: Manchuria and China, Ethiopia and Poland. The fact is, however, that the poorer countries occupy a large amount of the middle ground, the area in which the super-powers struggle for global advantage. Population pressures in the developing countries can and do have their impact on the major power conflict between the Eastern and Western blocs. On this point Richard M. Fagley makes a perceptive comment:

'The danger to peace in the underdeveloped world lies in the weakness of countries imbued with the hope of escape from ancient poverty and beset by mounting population pressures. Often without adequate indigenous leadership or any really dynamic international assistance, they struggle to keep their heads above water. But problems grow more rapidly than solutions, and encourage the dream of Communist empire. The temptations to Communist expansion and the last minute efforts of the West to prevent such expansion constitute the real dangers of war to which the population explosion is a major contributor.

'As matters now stand, with population growth rampant and tending to defeat even sacrificial efforts at economic development, the chief initial victim of the population explosion is likely to be the free society. No government in Asia can turn its back on the promise of economic and social progress which contacts with the West – including Christian missions – have helped to arouse. The level of international aid is thus far geared to a strategy which courts failure, at least in the densely populated countries. The amount of belt-tightening that is possible within the framework of a free society is limited, particularly in new democracies which cannot be expected to generate a high degree of self-discipline and sacrifice. Consequently, the tendency to abort and abandon the democratic experiment, in favour of a more coercive form of society, seems likely to grow, as indeed there is evidence in a number of countries. In most cases the authoritarian substitute may not take a Communist form. But the Soviet empire stands ready to harvest the failures. As I have argued before, the first issue in the lands of the population explosion is not economic and social development. The first issue is the free society.'[32]

How the poor live – and die

We have been looking at the question 'how many should we be?' as one which is of crucial importance, especially for the Christian, who, as we have reminded ourselves, must be concerned with the quality of life for all God's children. It has already proved impossible to talk about the question of quantity without referring also to the matter of quality.

For vast numbers of people life is little more than a struggle for survival: poverty, hunger and disease are the foundation stones of their grim prison-house of despair. Let us translate that general statement into concrete observation of one particular area. When I visited Haiti I was taken to see what must surely be one of the worst slums in the world. About 20,000 people live herded together in foul and squalid dwellings erected literally on a swamp. There is no running water and no sanitation. The homes of the people are constructed of bits of cardboard and rusty tin sheeting. Lean pigs and bedraggled hens scratch around among the heaps of evil-smelling rubbish that disfigure this place of human dereliction. As I picked my way gingerly through the drier parts of this miserable shanty town, sinking ankle deep in green sludge every so often, I found myself reciting 'I to the hills will life mine eyes From whence doth come my help'. But no, not there, certainly not there. For on the hills set against the deep blue sky are the white mansions of the wealthy who apparently neither see nor care. A little boy with bright eyes came up and said in broken English: 'Take me with you back to London'. But I stumbled away without him, overwhelmed by the magnitude of the misery of the world's poor. For you can multiply that little scene a million times.

The United Nations has identified the 'least developed countries'. They have a population of 258 millions (1977 estimate) – i.e. 13 per cent of the population of all developing countries. Their average income per head in 1977 was about £75. Over the past twenty years their slender per capita income has increased by less than one per cent. The situation of these countries is summarily described in the Brandt Report:

'Most of the least developed countries – the present U.N. list includes twenty-nine of them – are found contiguously in two areas which we call the "poverty belts". One extends across the middle of Africa, from the Sahara in the north to Lake Nyasa in the south. The other, beginning with the two Yemens and Afghanistan, stretches eastwards across South Asia and some East Asian countries. These belts extend into other regions and parts of countries, for example parts of Kenya in Africa and, in Asia, Burma, Cambodia, Vietnam and parts of India. The point has been raised whether parts of countries which have the same characteristics and handicaps as the least developed countries should not be treated on a par with them. The Commission hopes that the United Nations will continue to review its criteria and make consequential changes in the lists to ensure that they include all countries deserving special attention.

'Some of the countries in the poverty belts, like Bangladesh, have large populations; others such as Gambia are small in area and population. They each have different approaches to development; their economies have different degrees of openness. But each of them has a slim margin between subsistence and disaster; and they are all circumscribed by their ecology and their dependence on international market forces beyond their control. They exist in a fragile tropical environment which has been upset by the growing pressure of people. Without irrigation and water management, they are afflicted by droughts, floods, soil erosion and creeping deserts, which reduce the long-term fertility of the land. Disasters such as drought intensify the malnutrition and ill-health of their people and they are all affected by endemic diseases which undermine their vitality. Their poverty, harsh climate and isolation all make it harder to explore their resources, especially minerals. The sun, which might be a valuable source of cheap energy is presently a curse, sapping their vigour, while they are forced to use relatively expensive conventional forms of energy. They have to cut down their forests, degrading the environment in order to survive.

'This condition has worsened in the 1970s. Not only has the poorest countries' growth slowed down further; but even the increased assistance from the international community has been offset by a decline in the purchasing power of their exports. They also have had to face more starkly the grim possibility that their ecosystem may not enable them to feed their people – unless urgent measures are taken now.'[33]

There are those who believe that nothing can be done to stave off widespread famine and a catastrophic increase in all the accompanying miseries of disease and despair. This was the theme of the Paddock brothers in their book entitled 'Famine 1975!'. The only country with sufficient resources to give substantial aid, they argued, is the U.S.A. Even so it would have to employ the military method known as 'triage'.

' "Triage" is a term used in military medicine. It is defined as the assigning of priority of treatment to the wounded brought to a battlefield hospital in a time of mass casualties and limited medical facilities. The wounded are divided on the basis of three classifications:

1) Those so seriously wounded they cannot survive regardless of the treatment given them; call these the "can't-be-saved".

2) Those who can survive without treatment regardless of the pain they may be suffering; call these the "walking wounded".

3) Those who can be saved by immediate medical care.'[34]

'The triage principle is then applied to the war against hunger and nations divided into three groupings, as follows:

1) Nations in which the population growth trend has already passed the agricultural potential. This combined with inadequate leadership and other devisive factors make catastrophic disasters inevitable. These nations form the "can't-be-saved" group. To send food to them is to throw sand in the ocean.

2) Nations which have the necessary agricultural resources and/or foreign exchange for the purchase of food from abroad and which therefore will be able to cope with their population growth. They will be only moderately affected by the shortage of food. They are the "walking wounded" and do not require food aid in order to survive.

3) Nations in which the imbalance between food and population is great but the *degree* of the imbalance is manageable. Rather, it is manageable in the sense that it can give enough time to allow the local officials to initiate effective birth control practices and to carry forward agricultural research and other forms of development. These countries will have a chance to come through their crises provided careful medical treatment is given, that is, receipt of enough American food and also of other types of assistance.'[35]

Events have shown that the more disastrous prophecies of the Paddock brothers may yet be avoided but their well-documented study is a solemn warning to those who take the view that there is no need to worry as 'something will turn up'.

Whether something turns up or not depends upon the will to tackle the problems of a world in which for millions life is a struggle for survival.

Intermediate technology

One man who made a significant contribution to our thinking about how to assist developing countries was the late Dr. E. F. Schumacher. His work is being carried on by the Intermediate Technology Development Group in London. The fundamentals of his approach are set out in a paper which is included in his book 'Small is Beautiful':

'In many places in the world today the poor are getting poorer while the rich are getting richer, and the established processes of foreign aid and development planning appear to be unable to overcome this tendency. In fact, they often seem to promote it, for it is always easier to help those who can help themselves than to help the helpless. Nearly all the so-called developing countries have a modern sector where the patterns of living and working are similar to those of the developed countries, but they also have a non-modern sector, accounting for the vast majority of the total population, where the patterns of living and working are not only profoundly unsatisfactory but also in a process of accelerating decay.

'I am concerned here exclusively with the problem of helping the people in the non-modern sector. This does not imply the suggestion that constructive work in the modern sector should be discontinued, and there can be no doubt that it will continue in any case. But it does imply the conviction that all successes in the modern sector are likely to be illusory unless there is also a healthy growth – or at least a healthy condition of stability – among the very great numbers of people today whose life is characterised not only by dire poverty but also by hopelessness.'[36]

Dr. Schumacher goes on to describe how the task of bringing into existence millions of new work-places in rural areas and small towns might be accomplished. There are four requirements:

'*First*, that workplaces have to be created in the areas where the people are living now, and not primarily in metropolitan areas into which they tend to migrate.

Second, that these workplaces must be, on average, cheap enough so that they can be created in large numbers without this calling for an unattainable level of capital formation and imports.

Third, that the production methods employed must be relatively simple, so that the demands for high skills are minimised, not only in the production process itself but also in matters of organisation, raw material, supply, financing, marketing, and so forth.

Fourth, that production should be mainly from local materials and mainly for local use.

'These four requirements can be met only if there is a "regional" approach to development and, second, if there is a conscious effort to develop and apply what might be called an "intermediate technology".'[37]

This kind of intermediate technolgy – 'technology with a human face' – is now being widely employed. The emphasis on the person rather than the product makes an immediate appeal to Christians whose religion places such heavy stress on the value of the individual and the importance of true community.

Let the last word in this chapter be that of the Brandt Commission. It summarises its recommendations relating to the poorest countries in the following terms:

The Brandt recommendations

'An action programme must be launched comprising emergency and longer-term measures, to assist the poverty belts of Africa and Asia and particularly the least developed countries. Measures would include large regional projects of water and soil management; the provision of health care and the eradication of such diseases as river-blindness, malaria, sleeping sickness and bilharzia; afforestation projects; solar energy development; mineral and petroleum exploration; and support for industrialization, transport and other infrastructural investment.

'Such a programme would require additional financial

assistance of at least $4 billion per year for the next two decades, at grant or special concessional terms, assured over long periods and available in flexibly usable forms. New machinery is required on a regional basis to coordinate funding and to prepare plans in cooperation with lending and borrowing countries. Greater technical assistance should be provided to assist such countries with the preparation of programmes and projects.'[38]

Under the heading 'Disarmament and Development' the first and last paragraphs read:

'The public must be made more aware of the terrible danger to world stability caused by the arms race, of the burden it imposes on national economies, and of the resources it diverts from peaceful development.

'More research is necessary on the means of converting arms production to civilian production which could make use of the highly skilled scientific and technical manpower currently employed in arms industries.'[39]

Even a cursory examination of the immensity of the global problems confronting us is likely to raise in the minds of some the question whether there is really any hope for a world so beset. Are we not on a collision course with disaster; indeed does not the Christian religion teach that sin leads to destruction, and that all history moves to Armaggedon, the last great battle in which the wicked will perish, and the righteous will be saved, and Christ will establish his Kingly rule for ever? Is it not, therefore, futile for Christians to worry about the arms race and all the travail of a world that is doomed? All of which brings us to the pamphleteer who makes his appearance on the next page.

6: Refuge from the storm?

They have healed also the hurt of my people lightly, saying,
Peace, peace; when there is no peace.

Jeremiah 6:14

Encounter with a pamphleteer

London is a great place for pamphleteers. Most of the literature distributed free of charge on the city's pavements consists of advertisements for patent medicines, stylish clothes, cheap travel or the latest entertainment. The young man who approached me with a bag bulging with flysheets was, however, on more serious business. The tract he pressed into my hand was entitled 'Refuge from the storm!' It was badly printed and full of biblical quotations, but its message was clear. Briefly summarised it was this: the end of the world is imminent. The signs of the coming terror are clear enough: 'waste, pollution, over-population, starvation, monetary crisis, energy crisis, economic disaster, political chaos, the Arab-Israeli War, the final deflation of the Green Pig (America's worldwide dollar empire), the collapse and/or destruction of America, and finally World War Three!' However, there is a sure refuge from the storm for the pamphlet proceeds: 'You don't ever have to worry about it! And if God decides He'd rather *take* you than take *care* of you, why you've got it made, one way or the other. I mean, dead or alive, you're safe!'

The young man who gave me the tract had a kind face and was no doubt motivated by a genuine concern for his fellow-men. Yet I have to confess that I found the message he was asking me to accept false and even offensive.

The comfort of the scriptures

It is undeniably true that the bible speaks of God as sheltering those who put their trust in Him.

'You that live in the shelter of the Most High
and lodge under the shadow of the Almighty,
who say, "The Lord is my safe retreat
my God the fastness in which I trust",
he himself will snatch you away
from fowler's snare or raging tempest.
A thousand may fall at your side,
ten thousand close at hand,
but you it shall not touch'. (Psalm 91:1–3 and 7).

Why then should I find unacceptable a tract which stresses that when disaster comes 'the only truly safe place to be is in the Lord'? Have I not sung great hymns, like

'Rock of ages, cleft for me,
Let me hide myself in Thee'?

Is not the same sentiment the inspiration of other popular hymns like Isaac Watts' verses sung by large crowds on Armistice Day?

'O God, our help in ages past,
    Our hope for years to come,
Our shelter from the stormy blast,
    And our eternal home.'

Far from denying this authentic note of comfort which represents the experience of all true Christians, I affirm the reality of the fatherly love of God who cares for His children with tenderness and constancy.

Objections considered

My objections to the tract from which I have quoted are fourfold. First, its appeal seems to be a blatantly selfish one and suggests that the gospel is a kind of personal insurance policy or a way of securing a private dugout in which the believer can rest content even though the world outside is collapsing in ruin. This notion is entirely contrary to the unselfish service which, according to Jesus, is the hallmark of Christian discipleship. 'If anyone wishes to be a follower of mine, he must leave self behind; day after day he must take up his cross, and come with me' (Luke 9:23).

The second objection is that the tract makes no reference to the Christian vocation of peace-making. Salvation is seen as a plucking out of a world which is to be totally destroyed; the Christian has no responsibility *in* that world except to save his own skin. But the biblical roots of the word save suggest something very different. The Hebrew verb to save (*yasha*) – from which the name Jesus ('he who saves') is derived – means literally 'to be wide or spacious'. So the word *yasha* was used to represent the liberation of those who were confined. When Jesus began His ministry in Nazareth He read from Isaiah's prophecy:

'The spirit of the Lord is upon me because he has annointed me;
he has sent me to announce good news to the poor, to proclaim release for prisoners and recovery of sight for the blind;
to let the broken victims go free.'
(Luke 4:18–19)

The Greek word for salvation, *soteria*, does not do full justice to this concept for it is tinged with that idea of deliverance from bodily life which led to the extremes of ascetic renunciation which in no way reflected the life-affirming example of the Jesus who was criticised for eating with publicans and sinners. Christians are saved *for* the world rather than *from* it; they are to be the makers of peace. 'From first to last, this has been the work of God. He has reconciled us men to himself through Christ, and he has enlisted us in this service of reconciliation (2 Corinthians, 5:18).

The tract which I am criticising is open to a third objection. It is fatalistic. Fatalism assumes that the future can be known; indeed is already known. Nuclear holocaust is inevitable. The prospect is almost greeted with unholy relish as being the final demonstration of God's power and the divine judgement on an evil world. But the future is not predetermined. It has yet to be written. Christians are called not to a supine acceptance of evil and the inevitability of war, but to the patient and steady pursuit of peace. We are to 'seek peace and pursue it'. (1 Peter 3:11). We are bidden constantly to pray for peace: 'Persist in prayer . . . Call down blessings on your persecutors – blessings not curses'. (Romans 12:12 and 14). Whatever would be the point of praying for peace, if peace were impossible?

The reader may feel that we are spending too much time on a small tract distributed by an anonymous donor during a brief encounter on a busy London street. The reason for doing so, however, is that behind it stands a school of biblical interpretation which I believe to be mistaken and misleading. My fourth and weightiest objection, therefore, is that not only, as I have already said, is the biblical stress on peacemaking neglected, but the Bible is misused in such a way that the Church and its members are relieved of all responsibility for involvement in the effort to secure peace and avoid war. This is a very serious matter and must be dealt with before we proceed to consider in detail the Christian approach to the problems and opportunities of peacemaking.

Misuse of the Bible

The approach to the Bible which I describe as mistaken and misleading is expounded at some length in the writings of Hal Lindsey. In a book with the dramatic title 'The 1980's: Countdown to Armageddon' he refers to the reaction to an earlier treatise on the same theme:

'Shortly after *The Late Great Planet Earth* was published I began to see a most unusual phenomenon taking place. People from all walks of life were becoming captivated by an intense interest in the relevancy of the predictions made by the Hebrew prophets thousands of years ago.

'This interest wasn't confined to religious people, either. It extended all the way from college students to scientists to government officials both here and abroad.

'The interest also proved to have no geographical boundaries, as the book was translated into 31 foreign editions which were circulated in more than 50 countries. I began receiving letters and even phone calls literally from around the world.'[40]

The author proceeds with considerable ingenuity and inventiveness to relate biblical prophecies and particularly the apocalyptic passages in the Scriptures to the more disturbing events in the contemporary world. The rebirth of Israel, the alleged decline of American power and morality, the rise of Russian and Chinese might, the threat of war in the Middle East, the increase (real or supposed) of earthquakes, volcanic eruptions, famine and drought: all of these indicate that we will witness the end of the world and the return of Jesus.

Students of history – and even a little knowledge of history is an essential counterweight to extremist judgements – will know that there is nothing new about predictions of the sort just described. One of the astonishing aspects of human history is the recurrence of the delusion that the end of the world is imminent. Again and again some character has set himself or herself up as a prophet, and trading on the gullibility of others, as well as the motive of fear, has launched yet another sect centred on the belief that the end is at hand. Very often the actual date of this apocalyptic event has been confidently announced. So William Miller, an American Baptist minister, declared that he had discovered from the bible that the Lord would return in 1843. He later corrected this to 1844 but might have saved himself the trouble. Large numbers of people left their daily work to prepare for the great event. When nothing happened they were sadly disillusioned. Miller was the forerunner of Mrs. Ellen White who founded the Seventh-Day Adventist Movement. The Jehovah's Witnesses form another sect which subscribed to the slogan 'Millions now living will never die'. One of their recent forecasts was that the world would end in 1975. It did not, and neither did the Jehovah's Witnesses.

An approach to Apocalypse

I have already used the word 'apocalyptic'. It means 'pertaining to revelation' and is, in particular, the title of the last book of the Bible. There are many apocalyptic passages in the

Scriptures. They are distinguished by vivid language, and imagery of the kind which fills the Book of Revelation, and enshrine much of the eschatological teaching of the Bible (i.e. the teaching about the end, or the last things). Armageddon is the name given to what is seen in visionary fashion as the last great battlefield between good and evil. It probably contains a reference to the Hill (Hebrew = *Har*) of Megiddo in northern Palestine which was the scene of many decisive battles (e.g. 'Kings came, they fought, then fought the Kings of Canaan at Taanach by the waters of Megiddo'. Judges 5:19).

There is obviously no room to enter here upon a lengthy examination of this intriguing and often mystifying element in the Old and New Testaments. If, however, I have dismissed as mistaken and misleading a crude, literalistic, not to say highly subjective, interpretation of apocalyptic passages in the Bible, it is incumbent upon me to indicate in general how I believe they must be regarded.

My first comment is that the Bible is concerned with the beginning, the end, and everything in between. It is instructive to consider how the Bible deals with the beginning. The Book of Genesis opens with the sublime narrative of the creation. That narrative may be admired for its matchless prose and its poetic overtones. It may also be reverenced for its revelation of truth. But what sort of truth are we talking about? Not, I believe, historic truth and certainly not scientific truth, but rather that spiritual truth that can often best be conveyed in a story. Jesus Himself told many a story: we call them parables. To put it another way, the Genesis narrative of creation is full of brilliant imagery which mirrors the truth that God created the world and man in His own image. But just how the world came into being and what dates we are to attach to the various stages in the process is the concern of scientists who work within disciplines that simply did not exist when Genesis was written. In any case, when the scientists have told us all that they can about the beginning the mystery will still remain; indeed it will be deepened, for we are thinking of something which can only be hinted at in images.

What applies to the beginning applies also to the end. There must be an end: that stands to reason. When it will be and how it will happen we cannot know and it certainly is not our business to speculate. The one certainty for the Christian is that just as the beginning was in the hands of God and demonstrated His invincible power and love, so also will the end. That is all, and that is enough. The use of the highly-specialised thought-forms of a distant age as if they were a kind of Old Moore's Almanac is a dangerous misuse of Scripture. Hans Küng in his monumental study 'On being a Christian' states a position widely held by Christians throughout the world:

'Jesus naturally made use of the apocalyptic imagery and ideas of his own time. And even though – as we pointed out – he expressly rejected any exact calculations of the eschatological consummation and – by comparison with early Jewish apocalyptic – restricted to the utmost any picturesque description of the kingdom of God, in principle he remained within the framework of understanding of immediate expectation which seems strange to us today, within the horizon of apocalypticism. This framework of understanding has been rendered obsolete by historical developments, the apocalyptic horizon has been submerged: this must be clearly recognized. In the light of today's perspectives we have to say that what is involved in this immediate expectation is not so much an error as a time-conditioned, time-bound world view which Jesus shared with his contemporaries. It cannot be artificially reawakened. Nor indeed should the attempt be made to revive it for our very different horizon of experience, although there is always a temptation to do so particularly in what are known as "apocalyptic times". The apocalyptic framework of ideas and understanding of that time is alien to our mentality and today would only conceal and distort the reality behind it.'[41]

No road of escape

What, then, should be the Christian response to the dangers and difficulties which confront us today? It must be to take the creative task of positive peacemaking more seriously than ever before. Peace is the will of God. When Jesus was born the angels sang:

'Glory to God in highest heaven,
And on earth is peace, his favour towards men'

(Luke 2:14).

War is contrary to God's will. These are the basic convictions with which the Christian sets out to discover how he responds to the vocation to be a maker of peace. He may claim God's promised gift of peace for himself, and indeed he must for that is an essential prerequisite of effective peacemaking in the world. But that does not mean running away from the harsh realities of a world torn and divided by conflict. And most certainly it does not mean sitting down and waiting for the world to blow up as if that were inevitable and even part of the divine scheme of things. There is nothing inevitable about it at all. Christians are entrusted with a gospel of hope. Acceptance of the idea that a nuclear holocaust is inevitable cuts the nerve of that gospel and leaves us with nothing to say. For the Christian hope embraces this world and the next: both belong to God. Jesus bade us pray 'Thy Kingdom come on earth as it is in heaven'. A Church that is not challenging the drift towards war incessantly and persistently has abdicated its God-given responsibility; it is acquiescing in evil and has abandoned its belief in the power of goodness.

It is time we left our pamphleteer though not without gratitude for the challenge his appearance in our pages presents. Since the Christian religion offers us no escape route from responsibility we must look more closely at the Church's attitude. How has this been traditionally understood and what new factors now call for a reassessment of established positions? These are the matters to which we turn in the next chapter.

7: The Church and violence

> *From first to last this has been the work of God. He has reconciled us men to himself through Christ, and he has enlisted us in this service of reconciliation.*

2 Corinthians, 5:18

A backward glance

Ecclesia abhorret a sanguine – the Church shrinks from bloodshed. That is true enough, but Christians have inherited a somewhat ambivalent tradition on the matter of the use of violence. An indiscriminate appeal to biblical texts can win support for almost any view one cares to suggest. The Old Testament contains plenty of examples of bloody warfare undertaken at the direct command of the Lord. 'The Lord said to Joshua, "Do not be fearful or dismayed; take the whole army and attack Ai. I deliver the King of Ai into your hands, him and his people, his city and his country".' (Joshua 8:1). The narrative goes on to indicate that the whole population of Ai, twelve thousand in all, were slaughtered. The King was captured and brought to Joshua who hanged him from a tree. The whole enterprize was considered to be a good day's work for the Lord.

It is quite impossible to make anything of the Bible as a book of moral and spiritual guidance unless one recognizes that it is a record of progress in understanding as God educated His people and enabled them to see more of the truth. By the time we reach the end of the Old Testament various views were held on the subject of violence. Many were looking for a Messiah who would by military might overcome all Israel's enemies and establish her as a super power. But there were others who dreamed of a different destiny. Their thinking is movingly expressed in Isaiah's prophecy where he speaks of the Suffering Servant. Does the prophet refer to Israel or to some personification of Israel or to a particular person? It does not really matter. The emphasis is on the power of suffering love to heal and save. Some of the words describe with penetrating accuracy and haunting beauty the example of our Lord though His birth, life and death still lay in the distant future:

'he was pierced for our transgressions,
tortured for our iniquities;
the chastisement he bore is health for us
and by his scourging we are healed.
He was afflicted, he submitted to be struck down
and did not open his mouth;
he was led like a sheep to the slaughter.'

(Isaiah 53:5 and 7).

By the time we reach the period covered by the gospels the Jewish people are under Roman rule. The Zealots were, as we should say, the freedom fighters of that time. They were committed to the overthrow of their foreign rulers by violent means. One member of this party is named among the twelve disciples of Jesus ('Simon who was called the Zealot', Luke 6:15). It may be that Judas Iscariot was a rather extreme member of the same group and that his betrayal of Jesus was due to irritation with the Master's patience and forbearance which he would see as failure to act decisively in the only way that would further the cause of Jewish independence.

It is not possible from the records we have to tell exactly how much influence the Zealots had on the followers of Jesus. Certainly the disciples often talked as though they thought in terms of national supremacy as the fulfilment of God's will: 'Lord, is this the time when you are to establish once again the sovereignty of Israel?' (Acts 1:6). Jesus, however, quite deliberately cast Himself in the role of the Suffering Servant: 'he began to teach them that the Son of Man had to undergo great sufferings, and to be rejected by the elders, chief priests, and doctors of the law; to be put to death, and to rise again three days afterwards'. (Mark 8:31–2). When all of this began to happen and Jesus was paraded before Pilate, He said 'My Kingdom does not belong to this world. If it did, my followers would be fighting'. (John 18:36).

There can be little doubt that the early Christians regarded military service as inconsistent with their profession as followers of Jesus. For nearly three hundred years the Christian Church was virtually pacifist. But the position changed when, following the conversion of Constantine, Christianity was accepted as the principal state religion. Though there were exceptions Christians generally came to the view that they had a duty to defend the state against attack, so increasing numbers of them became soldiers. However, in the fourth century Eusebius, a Christian teacher of Caesarea, insisted that the clergy should be exempt from military service. Augustine of Hippo, (354–430 A.D.), a great theologian, laid the foundations for the Christian doctrine of the just war. Christians were justified in going to war in order to prevent further conflict and in pursuit of justice. He also argued that it was quite possible to preserve an inward temper of meekness and charity even when engaged on the regrettable but necessary business of killing the enemy.

The history of the succeeding centuries reveals the way in which honest Christians struggled with the problems of reconciling the call of Christ to personal standards of peacemaking with the responsibilities which result from our corporate membership of the state. But that same history also demonstrates the constant erosions brought about by compromise. Not only was it regarded as right to defend one's country by force of arms, but also to defend one's beliefs. During the Crusades the justification for armed violence was extended further to embrace attacks upon those regarded as infidels.

The just war doctrine

Pacifist and Non-Pacifist Views

The way in which many modern Christians now see the matter is admirably set forth in an official declaration of the Methodist Church:

'The Mind of our Lord

We acknowledge that war is contrary to the spirit, teaching and purpose of our Lord. The simple, yet all comprehending, command He laid upon those who follow Him,

that they should love God and should love their neighbour, shattered all narrower limitations and extended the
obligation of love and charity to include the stranger and
the enemy. He Himself met evil with good, hatred with love,
and persistent injury with persistent readiness to forgive. He
faced the world with unfailing and unyielding goodness,
teaching men, both by precept and example, to love their
enemies. He forgave those who wronged Him even unto death.

'We believe that His teaching and example were intended
to apply not only to individual relations, but to the social and
corporate affairs of men, and to the intercourse of nations. If
the prayer, "Thy kingdom come", is ever to be finally and
fully realised on earth it can only be in a world-embracing
brotherhood of righteousness, love and peace. Since the
causes of war are ultimately to be found in the unregenerate
hearts and uncontrolled passions of mankind, the Conference
calls the Methodist people, in their service for peace, to
unwearied devotion in witness to the redemptive power of
Christ and to a life of love and charity with their neighbours,
rendering to no man evil for evil, but striving to overcome
evil with good.

'The Christian Attitudes to War

We must, however, face the fact that there is division of
judgement among earnest and convinced Christians concerning the application of these generally accepted principles to
the harsh realities of the present situation. All Christians
agree that war is evil. Some believe that it is, therefore, in
every circumstance to be rejected by the follower of Christ.
Others believe that there are situations in which the waging of
war is inevitable as the choice of the lesser of two admitted
evils.

'(i) Christian Pacifism

The Christian pacifist case is rooted in a theological interpretation of the Cross, and an acceptance of the practical
obligations to act on that belief. It is a faith in the power of
God to achieve His purpose through human obedience to the
Cross of Jesus Christ as the instrument of salvation. Jesus
taught that we must love our enemies. He Himself loved his
enemies with such complete dedication that for their sakes

He deliberately laid down His life. His teaching, exemplified in His life and supremely validated by His death on the Cross, was that the way of God is the way of love, conversion and reconciliation. This He practised, no matter what the cost to Himself or to others. Those who have become reconciled to God through Christ are called to follow this way.

'It is of the essence of war that it involved the deliberate and intentional killing of other human beings. The pacifist does not condemn the use of any and every kind of force. Any penal action requires force of some kind, and force can be used in many ways that are entirely beneficent. A restraining force used against a criminal which still leaves open the way towards his reform is an acceptable use of force. But to employ it of set intention for the destruction of others is altogether unacceptable. It is true that war lays upon the participants the readiness to die, but it is not, therefore, necessarily to be equated with sacrifice. For these reasons the Christian pacifist believes that participation in war is incompatible with his obedience.

'The appalling developments of modern warfare – mass destruction, bacteriological warfare, indiscriminate attack – underline and emphasize its horrors, and may, therefore, the more clearly expose the sinfulness of war, but they do not modify or affect the fundamental theological argument. If war were to be "civilized", restricted only to combatants, and waged under agreed conventions that would limit the grosser barbarities of nuclear warfare, it would still be wrong.

'It is the duty, and the privilege, of the Christian not to be overcome of evil, but to overcome evil with good.

'(ii) *Christian Non-Pacifism*

The Christian non-pacifist conviction is also rooted in a theology of the Cross. Abhorring war and the evils that stem from it, the non-pacifist rejects absolute pacifism because he believes that it obscures the Christian concept of love and tries to apply an individual ethic to a collective situation. Love, which manifests itself in self-sacrificial service, manifests itself also in a concern for social justice. In a sinful world, there are occasions when the claims of peace and justice conflict and a choice must be made. Both the struggle for justice and the struggle for peace present a moral imperative, but justice has the prior claim, for there can be no lasting peace without it. The non-pacifist argues that the triumph of an unjust cause would defeat both the ends of justice and the hope of peace. The non-pacifist hesitates to arrogate to himself as a follower of Christ all the attributes of his Lord. The Cross and the Resurrection were the divinely ordained means of our salvation, but a means which derived their saving power from the fact that it was Christ who died and rose again. The problem with which the Christian non-pacifist wrestles is that of the victims of aggression. His motive is not self-preservation. He would be prepared to offer himself if that would ensure their salvation. It will not. If he, by his conscience, is prohibited from defending them, are they to be left defenceless?

'The Christian non-pacifist does not justify every war. He is, indeed, a reluctant upholder of defensive warfare within very narrowly defined limits. But believing that God wills both justice and peace, he is not prepared to agree that invariably and inevitably pacifism is the will of God.'[42]

One constant feature of the changing attitude of the Church to armed conflict has been the insistence on limiting the scale of violence permitted. Some interesting rulings have been laid down indicating the somewhat tortuous devices to which moral theologians resort. For example, the Second Lateran Council in 1139 banned the use of crossbows, bows and arrows, and siege machines against Christians (what, one wonders, was left in the way of weaponry?), but permitted their employment against infidels and heretics.

The doctrine of the just war was refined and restated. In its fullest form its essential features are that for a war to be deemed justifiable it must:

1. have been undertaken by a lawful authority;
2. have been undertaken for the vindication of an undoubted right that had been certainly infringed;
3. be a last resort, all peaceful means of settlement having failed;
4. offer the possibility of good to be achieved outweighing the evils that war would involve;
5. be waged with a reasonable hope of victory for justice;
6. be waged with a right intention;

7. use methods that are legitimate, i.e. in accordance with man's nature as a rational being, with Christian moral principles and international agreements.

Whether always fully understood or not, this is the formula which has undergirded the decision of Christians to participate in war, or at least not to resist the requirement of the state upon them to do so.

A new situation

We now have to ask whether the Christian doctrine of the just war can be applied in any meaningful way to nuclear warfare waged with megaton weapons. There surely can be no doubt about the answer. It cannot. Consider the conditions numbered (4), (5) and (7). It is not possible to believe that any good achieved would outweigh the evils that such a war would involve. Popular assertions like 'We'd rather be dead than red', even if they in any way reflect the real options, are superficial and result from a failure actually to contemplate the enormity of the destruction which nuclear war would let loose. There certainly can be no victory for anyone in a nuclear war, only defeat for all that is good and worth preserving. By no twist of argument or stretch of imagination can it be supposed that nuclear warfare fought with megaton weapons accords with man's nature as a rational being, or with Christian moral principles and international agreements.

The recognition that the nuclear age is in every sense, including moral sense, a new age has not yet full registered in the minds and consciences of many. As we noted on p. 20, there are some who argue that there is nothing essentially new about the situation. This has always been a violent world, they argue: once men killed with slings and stones, then with bows and arrows, small guns and bigger ones, modest bombs and monstrous missiles. It is only the scale of destruction that has changed. But there comes a point where quantitative developments require new qualitative responses. The recognition of this is implicit in the understanding of the methods of moral theology which produced the doctrine of the just war.

If the Christian doctrine of the just war cannot in any way

be tailored to provide justification for the use of massive nuclear weapons, there could still conceivably be a situation in which the use of smaller so-called field, theatre or tactical nuclear missiles could be justified along the lines of the traditional argument. But that way of thinking is perilous. Whilst no-one can be certain, it is at least very likely that in a war situation the scale of violence would escalate, as has happened in previous conflicts, and so the use of smaller nuclear weapons would lead to the employment of the monsters which can annihilate whole populations. (See the judgement of the late Professor Burhop quoted on p. 59).

Is it then now the universally held view among all Christians that nuclear weapons are totally inadmissible and that no Christian justification can be advanced in support of them? The answer to that question is 'No' and the reason for this is the persuasive strength, as some see it, of the deterrent argument. Because the theory of nuclear deterrence has dominated so much recent discussion and because it undergirds the military policy of both West and East we must examine it with care and at some length.

The deterrent argument

During a visit I paid to a famous naval establishment I was invited to meet a number of senior officers with responsibility for the handling of nuclear weapons. I was asked to set out my views and then to listen to their response. With great courtesy they explained their understanding of the policy of the British government. They were at pains to stress that the whole object of possessing nuclear weapons was to ensure that they are never used. They explained that the slogan etched on their minds is 'If we fire, we've lost'.

The theory of deterrence was expounded with characteristic clarity by the British Foreign and Commonwealth Secretary, Lord Carrington, in his Churchill Memorial Lecture delivered in Luxembourg on the 27th October, 1981:

'The record shows that the Soviet Union is willing to use force. We have seen it in Hungary and Czechoslovakia. We are seeing it now in Afghanistan. But we have not seen it so far in Western Europe. Why this difference? We cannot tell for certain what Soviet intentions have been, are or will be in future. It may be that the Soviet Union has no aggressive intentions. But we cannot afford to take risks, and common prudence requires us to assume that the difference may have been quite simply that the risks have been too great.

'That brings me to the concept of deterrence – of possessing weapons to prevent war. It is a difficult concept, often stated and rarely explained. How is the basic argument to be re-stated with an immediacy that the young man or woman in the street will feel and comprehend?

'He who will not learn the lessons of history is condemned to re-live them. That is certainly a principle that Churchill understood. Political debate today too often lacks historical perspective. For 2,000 years the experience of the peoples of Europe has been to live and re-live the lesson that the price of freedom is untiring vigilance. A first duty of the State is to ensure protection from external assault. Why should it be any different today? Observing the behaviour of the most powerful State on the Eurasian landmass since 1945, do we have any reason to suppose that Western security can be left to look after itself? I think the answer is self-evident. I am reminded of that wry East European joke which says, by way of excuse for the hardships of everyday life, "We are going through a bad 500 years just now". I never wish to see Western Europe obliged to fall back on such dark humour.

'Nuclear weapons have transformed our view of war. But abhorrence of war is no substitute for realistic plans to prevent it. Our task is to devise a system for living in peace and freedom while ensuring that nuclear weapons are never used, either for destruction or for blackmail.

'Nuclear weapons dominate the discussion today. But we tend conveniently to forget that some 50 million people died in World War II, killed by what are comfortably called conventional weapons. Since 1945 conventional war has killed up to 10 million more. We in Europe, to ensure our security, must prevent *any* East-West war. The combination of geography and totalitarian control of resources gives the Soviet Union a massive conventional strength which the Western democracies have chosen not to match. And even if they were to, no Western non-nuclear effort could keep us safe against one-sided Soviet nuclear power.

'The purpose of deterrence is to influence the calculations

of anyone who might consider an attack, or the threat of an attack, against us; to influence them before any such attack is ever launched; and to influence them decisively. Planning for this means thinking through the possible reasoning of an adversary. It means trying to ensure that he could not see a possibility of depriving the West of all alternatives but surrender. Failure to recognise this complicated but crucial fact about deterrence – that it rests on blocking off in advance a variety of possible moves in an opponent's mind – underlies many of the criticisms made of Western security policy. To do this is not in the least to have a "war fighting strategy" or to plan for nuclear war as something expected or probable. It is, on the contrary, to ensure that, even if an adversary believed in limited nuclear war, as Soviet writings sometimes suggest, he could not expect actually to engage in one without losses out of all proportion to the desired gains.

'N.A.T.O., then, is there to deter a possible adversary from starting a war, by making sure that the risk will always be too high. The East-West peace has held for 36 years now, a peace between political systems that are sharply opposed and powers that have innumerable points of possible friction. That is a striking achievement in the European historical perspective. No-one can *prove* that deterrence centred on nuclear weapons has played a key part; but commonsense suggests that it must have done and it would be lunacy to assert that it had not.

'Our purpose today is to *maintain* peace. That brings me back to the Soviet military build-up. Chancellor Schmidt is right when he stresses the importance of military balance. The danger today is that the imbalances that have developed will undermine deterrence. The erosion of deterrence would reduce the risks facing a potential aggressor and thus *increase* the chance of war. The many honest people in Europe who oppose nuclear weapons, and those in my country who advocate unilateral disarmament, are mistaken because of one fundamental fact: what they are suggesting would make war *more* likely.'[43]

Lord Carrington does not suggest that deterrence by itself is an adequate policy in East-West relations. Indeed he urges the need to work unremittingly for effective arms control, improved trade and cultural relations and measures aimed at reducing tension. Nevertheless he is a firm exponent of deterrence and expresses his opposition to those who in increasing numbers demonstrate against nuclear weapons.

The case against the deterrent argument

I have already remarked on the fact that the theory of nuclear deterrence undergirds the military policy of both West and East. On both sides the case for building up the weapons of war as an essential guarantee of peace is advanced with apparently deep conviction. Not infrequently it is suggested that those who reject this concept are 'naive'. This is a word which is often used by those who wish to dismiss arguments that they cannot answer. The case against the deterrent argument is, however, a weighty one. Consider the following points:

a) *A proposition which can't be proved*

Lord Carrington says that 'the East-West peace has held for 36 years now'. (It is, perhaps, worth noting yet again how words are abused. There may not have been armed conflict in Europe over that period, and for this we should be grateful, but a state of dangerously armed antagonism can scarcely be described as 'peace': cold war is a far more apt description). He goes on to say that 'no-one can *prove* that deterrence centred on nuclear weapons has played a key part'. That is undoubtedly true. No-one can be sure what part nuclear weapons have played. Deterrence is a theory that can neither be proved nor disproved. Therefore the basis of the argument is one of speculation, not of certainty. Many of the protagonists of nuclear deterrence seem to have forgotten that.

b) *The increasing danger of war by accident*

The danger of accidental nuclear war increases. Bland assurances that the built-in checks and safety measures are so numerous and effective that no-one need worry must be regarded as eye-wash. So long as technology involves fallible men there will always be the chance of accident, and there are no infallible men. We are sometimes told that, of course, 'the best brains' are in charge of advanced nuclear weaponry, but little comfort can be derived from that when one considers the history of military catastrophes. The Teheran hostage rescue effort was no doubt devised and presided over by the best brains but it was an unmitigated disaster.

There have been a number of occasions when the public has been made aware of technical defects in defence machinery. The Pentagon in the U.S.A. estimates that during the 1970s each of its early-warning systems gave a false signal about once every three months. Increasing sophistication of technology means greater vulnerability both to mechanical flaws and human errors.

The sheer weight of responsibility for controlling weapons with monstrous destructive capacity imposes unique strain on those involved. In the year 1972 about 200,000 people in the U.S.A. came into this category. Of these 3,650 were dismissed because of some form of instability: mental illness, alcohol or drug abuse, or indiscipline. Dervla Murphy makes this comment:

'In America each Titan silo is guarded by two armed men, capable of launching the missile, who must spend long hours in a confined space. Each has orders to shoot the other if he shows the slighest sign of abnormal behaviour and more than thirty Titan guards have been seriously psychologically disturbed since those missiles were first deployed.

'Writing in the *Guardian* on 9 October 1975, Jonathan Steele reported that at one site near Omaha, Nebraska, a young officer said: "We have two tasks. The first is not to let people go off their rockers. That's the negative side. The positive one is to ensure that people act without moral compunction". In a few words, that young man summed up our civilisation's collapse. Suddenly, reading them, I.M.P. (Industrial/Military/Political monolith) appears naked – with no "just war" figleaf – as the instrument of Evil. And one remembers E. P. Thompson's diagnosis: "Deterrence is not a stationary state, it is a degenerative state." '[44]

c) *The perils of proliferation*

The next point concerns the dangers of nuclear proliferation. In spite of what has just been said about the effects of stress on some of those involved in the handling of nuclear weapons, it is commonly assumed that 'the men at the top' (and, of course, the women) are basically of sound mind and highly rational. The protagonists of deterrence may imply that Soviet leaders are a wicked lot with sinister intentions, but the basic rationality of those leaders is not questioned; rather the contrary, for the deterrent threat would obviously not work if it were directed against people who were incapable of grasping the point. It is further assumed that the leaders of any nation that was sophisticated enough to have been able to produce a nuclear bomb would have attained to a similar level of rationality. That comfortable illusion is dispelled by Norman Moss:

'We live now with the danger of nuclear war. If more nations have nuclear weapons, then the number of possible nuclear wars will increase. Some people have suggested that once a nation has reached the state of scientific and technological development needed to produce nuclear weapons, then it will have attained a level of safely rational behaviour, that an Idi Amin with an atomic bomb is a nightmare that could not come true. This idea might have afforded some comfort if the years between 1933 and 1945 had not shown what can happen to a scientifically and industrially advanced country.

'In fact, a number of Third World countries might be more prone to use nuclear weapons than the present possessors. For one thing, they have a lower threshold of conflict. It is hard to imagine any of the major powers going to war with another over the kind of territorial claim that led to the Iraq-Iran War. For another, in those parts of the world where nations are newer, and territorial boundaries less firmly fixed by the weight of centuries, there are more potential causes for conflict in ethnic discontent, where a group of people decides it does not belong in the nation to which the decolonizing process assigned it. For another, there has grown up among the five nuclear powers a nuclear taboo: a tacit understanding that the threshold between conventional weapons and any kind of nuclear weapon, of whatever explosive power, is to be crossed only *in extremis*, because this opens the way to nuclear escalation with no further barrier in sight. A new nuclear power might not draw the same distinction between nuclear weapons and other weapons.

'In discussion of the possible spread of nuclear weapons, some people draw consolation from the fact that a new nuclear weapons state would almost certainly produce fission bombs, with a low yield of 'only' 10 or 20 kilotons, not the multi-megaton hydrogen bombs, which require a much greater scientific/technological effort to build, and which in their thousands make up the nuclear arsenals of the super-powers. This only shows how the imagination, not to say the conscience, has been dulled by the war talk of the nuclear age.'[45]

Mention has already been made (pp. 56, 73) of the fact that a number of militarily significant countries have not signed the Non-Proliferation Treaty. Many of these have nuclear energy programmes and could easily qualify for membership of what has been rather objectionably called 'the nuclear club'. India is a particularly interesting example. It is one of the world's poorest countries with the second largest population. But it has always had a Western-educated élite which has held the reigns of government and exercised enormous power. This is the reason why India has been able to develop high tech-nology industries. On the morning of Saturday, 14th May, 1974, the Indians exploded a nuclear device in the Rajasthan Desert. The pre-arranged signal delivered to Prime Minister Indira Gandhi to indicate that the explosion had been suc-cessfully carried out was 'The Buddha smiles'. It would be difficult to think of a less appropriate image unless, perhaps, the one sent to President Truman following the dropping of the atom bomb on Hiroshima. 'Baby born on schedule'. How true it is that 'Satan himself masquerades as an angel of light' (2 Corinthians 11:14). It comes as no surprise that the U.S. Atomic Energy Commission called the strontium 90 radioac-tive fallout from nuclear bomb tests 'Project Sunshine'.

The Indian government insisted that the Rajasthan ex-plosion was part of the development of its atoms for peace programme. In India itself there was widespread welcome for the news though elsewhere in the world the reaction was shock and alarm. It was now clear beyond a doubt that any country with a nuclear reactor and a reprocessing plant could produce an explosive device. By 1985 some forty countries will have nuclear energy programmes and the number will continue to grow. By 1990 in the Third World alone reactors could be producing enough nuclear material for 3,000 Hiroshima-sized bombs a year.

Whatever may be said about the deterrent argument in the past it looks less and less plausible as one considers the nightmare possibility of nuclear bombs everywhere in the future.

d) *Changes in military doctrine*

We must now consider the fact that military nuclear doctrine has been changing. New terms keep entering into the vocabulary of discussion, like 'pre-emptive first strike', 'counterforce' and 'flexible response'. What, in fact, has been happening is not that American and Soviet politicians have ordered new types of nuclear weapons for political purposes; rather is it the case that uncontrolled military technology has produced the weapons and then policies have been modified to rationalise their deployment.

The idea of a pre-emptive first strike is that in a tense international situation, when one side believed that the other was planning a surprise attack aimed at disabling their enemy, the nation which believed itself threatened would make the first move. The increasing accuracy of delivery systems seems to give a certain plausibility to this notion, but the enormous dangers implicit in such an action, if ever it were undertaken, are clear enough.

Even while this book is being written there has been more and more talk about the possibility of a limited nuclear war in Europe. Ambivalent and contradictory statements from American officials have caused a rash of alarmed and angry comment. Anti-nuclear demonstrations have been taking place on an unprecedented scale. On October 10th 1981 250,000 people gathered in Bonn to protest. Over the weekend of October 24–25 1981 there were marches by 300,000 in Rome, 250,000 in London, 200,000 in Brussels, 50,000 in Paris and 7,000 in Oslo. These demonstrations were organised and supported by religious leaders, youth, trade union and political organisations. They were protesting at the Soviet Union's SS20 missiles and at the 1979 N.A.T.O. decision to place 572 new Cruise and Pershing missiles in sites in N.A.T.O. countries.

Dr. Frank Barnaby, Director of the Stockholm International Peace Research Institute, comments that any policy based on nuclear weapons must be irrational and that this is particularly obvious when one considers Europe:

'Soviet and American views differ on when and how

tactical nuclear weapons would be used in a European war. N.A.T.O.'s plans for the defence of Europe, though, are based on an awesome bluff. On the one hand, N.A.T.O. says that a significant attack by the Warsaw Treaty Organization (W.T.O.), even if non-nuclear, would be countered with nuclear weapons. But this would set in motion a series of events leading to the certain destruction of most European cities, and the death of most of its people.

'No sane European political leader would be willing deliberately to initiate such a chain of events. But the public admission of such unwillingness would, it is said, "undermine the credibility of the deterrent". The belief is that this would increase the probability of an attack.

'Nevertheless, there doubtless are (or will be) some irrational political and military leaders who actually *would* destroy Europe in order to save it. And if such people should have their fingers on the trigger at the crucial moment, they might bring about a nuclear holocaust. In short, N.A.T.O.'s bluff could be called and Europe could be utterly destroyed.'[46]

Barnaby goes on to argue that the introduction of very low-yield nuclear weapons would blur the present distinction between conventional and nuclear weapons. He adds that it is of the greatest importance to maintain an absolute 'firebreak' between nuclear and conventional war and concludes:

'I go even further than those who believe that a war in which any nuclear weapons are used will escalate all the way to a nuclear world war in which all, or the bulk, of the nuclear weapons in the arsenals are used. I believed that *any* war in Europe would escalate in this way. In other words, any significant hostile action across the German border is, in my opinion, almost bound to escalate to a nuclear world war. To believe otherwise is to believe that one side will surrender while it still has a large arsenal left. Those that have experienced war in Europe know that countries at war do not surrender under these conditions, particularly when emotions are as high as they are in the midst of a violent war.

'The only sensible policy for the nuclear weapons powers is to reduce their nuclear arsenals as a step to the total abolition of nuclear weapons.'[47]

There are signs that the rapidly developing peace movements and the manifest evidence of public concern have begun to impinge on the consciousness of political leaders. At the end of November 1981 President Brezhnev travelled to West Germany to confer with Chancellor Schmidt on the eve of renewed arms control talks between the two superpowers in Geneva. Both sides in the talks have tried to score propaganda points against each other. The correspondence columns of the newspapers have carried letters arguing the need for further strengthening of the forces of the Western Allies in order to achieve or maintain the military balance between East and West. Much of this argument is completely pointless. Figures quoted by both sides can be used to support almost any point of view. The inescapable fact is that both East and West have enough nuclear fire-power to destroy civilization as we know it and to do it many times over. Public pressure to reduce and then eliminate nuclear weapons as first steps in a continuing programme of progressive disarmament must be resolutely maintained.

e) *Assumptions about Soviet policy*

In spite of what has just been said about the idea of military 'balance' the momentum of the arms race has been maintained and indeed increased, so far as the West is concerned by the constant reiteration of the allegation that we live under the shadow of 'the Soviet threat'. The Western arms programme is said to be a regrettable necessity forced upon us by the massive build-up of Soviet forces since World War II. The sinister intentions of the Russians are underlined by their military interventions, especially in Eastern Europe.

If anyone in the West attempts to criticise this current orthodoxy or plead for a less one-sided assessment he is almost certain to be labelled 'pro-communist' or unpatriotic, or, deadliest indictment of all, just naive. However, Christians at any rate are in business to try to counter false propaganda of whatsoever kind, and to search out the truth, even when others do not wish to hear it. Part of the danger of our contemporary situation is that to a degree rarely recognised we are all the victims of our own propaganda. Christians, claiming as they do to be members of the only truly supranational body, should be capable of taking a broader view than that which is dictated merely by nationalistic prejudices. I say they should be able to do so, though the difficulties are enormous. I recall the way in which this realization was driven home upon my own mind at the Fifth Assembly of the World Council of Churches in Nairobi. When discussing international questions representatives of the Western Churches were heard to complain that their friends from the Russian Orthodox Church were obviously peddling Soviet government propaganda. It seemed equally obvious to the Russian Church leaders that their friends from the West were unduly influenced by the imperialism of their capitalist mentors.

It is instructive and helpful to read some of the assessments that emanate from neutral observers who have no commitment to either power bloc. It is no part of my intention to offer excuses for the massive, dangerous and wickedly wasteful build-up of arms by either East or West. If, however, there is to be an informed public opinion exercising increasing pressure for sensible disarmament proposals, it is important to try to achieve a greater degree of understanding than can be gained from the superficial propaganda pumped out by both sides.

It is not at all difficult to understand why many in the West fear the Russians. Christians must never forget that there are large numbers of faithful believers in the Soviet Union, and that they have suffered grievous persecution. I have been the guest of both Orthodox and Baptist Christians in Russia and found their devotion to our common Lord a deeply moving experience. Nevertheless the prevailing philosophy of the rulers of Russia is atheistic communism. The freedom of the individual is severely limited and dissidents are often hounded and persecuted. Not only so, but there is a missionary fervour about the communist creed and those who are committed to it are eager to extend its influence. When, therefore, we see on our television screens the May Day parade in Red Square and the cavalcade of weaponry streaming past Lenin's tomb topped by the sombre faces of the leaders of that vast country, a shudder of dismay is a perfectly understandable reaction. Those same leaders are always asserting that their military strength is entirely in the interests of defence, and weapons expenditure a regrettable necessity forced on them by the aggressive tendencies of the

Western powers, particularly America, but we do not trust them. In fact Soviet weapons with immense destructive potential are actually trained on our centres of population. In the light of all that there are even some who say 'We'd rather be dead than red'.

What sort of picture emerges if we make an honest attempt to imagine how things look to a Soviet military planner? It cannot be denied that the world must seem to be a very dangerous place indeed. The Soviet Union, unlike the U.S.A., is literally surrounded by hostile powers and somewhat unreliable allies. She has an enormous border to defend: the one with China is the longest in the world. In the last war Russia suffered 20 million dead and the most appalling devastation of her land and economy. The aging leaders of the U.S.S.R. do not forget that China's leaders regard the Soviet Union as representing the chief threat to their security, but equally Russia fears China (whose population is four times as large and whose military potential is very considerable). When Russia looks at America her view is very different from ours. She sees a country with enormous wealth and technical efficiency controlled by a political system she regards as corrupt. She is able to point to the fact that America was the first to get the atom bomb and that she has led the way in virtually every qualitative and quantitative advance in the arms race. No doubt the military significance of Britain does not loom very large in Soviet thinking since the days of our imperial expansion are now far behind us; but America is a different matter. She has intervened militarily or through her intelligence agencies in Indochina, the Dominican Republic, Chile, Iran and elsewhere. Moreover the U.S.A. maintains an enormous global network of military bases in Europe, Turkey, Korea, the Philippines, Okinawa and Japan. There has been no pledge by the U.S.A. not to be the first to use nuclear weapons. Russia fears and distrusts the West. So long as there is an arms race she will make every effort to keep up or even forge ahead of her potential adversaries.

f) Considerations of moral theology

So far I have been building up the case against the deterrent argument mainly on the basis of what might be called 'practical politics'. This is the level at which intelligent discussion of the issue usually takes place. But for the Christian there is and must be another dimension to the argument. What he believes generally about life and the way it is to be lived must be grounded in sound theology. What he believes about the rights and wrongs of particular issues must be determined by sound moral theology. I have argued earlier in this chapter that Christian moral theology provides no justification for the use of nuclear weapons of mass destruction. Since, however, many of the protagonists of deterrence, as we have seen, claim that the whole point of possessing these weapons is to ensure that they are never used, we must ask what moral theology has to say about the morality of possessing nuclear weapons.

It is a basic principle of Christian morality that, if it is wrong to do a particular thing, it is wrong also to intend to do it. So Jesus says: 'You have learned that you were told, "Do not commit adultery". But what I tell you is this: If a man looks on a woman with a lustful eye, he has already committed adultery with her in his heart' (Matthew 5:27-8). The intention to do a wrong thing is as morally reprehensible as the doing of it.

Those who wish to defend the concept of deterrence may respond in some such fashion as this: 'It is overstating the matter to say that it is our intention to drop nuclear bombs. In fact our intention is really quite the opposite. As we keep saying, our aim, indeed our intention, is to prevent such horrible weapons ever being used. It is only our intention to use them if they are first used against us'. The reply to that is that if the dropping of nuclear bombs is absolutely wrong, then it is wrong in all circumstances, and wrong to intend to do it whatever the situation may be.

There is, however, another line of argument which the protagonist of deterrence might take. He might argue: 'I am wholly convinced that the use of nuclear bombs in any circumstances is wrong, and that Christians cannot possibly justify their deployment for any reason whatsoever. I accept, too, that if a thing is wrong so also is the intention to do it. But the truth is that there is no intention to use nuclear weapons. It is entirely right, and unfortunately absolutely necessary to _have_ these weapons. Our very strong hope is that no hostile power would ever run the risk of the damaging retaliation we could inflict if we were attacked. But we should not retaliate. If we were subjected to a nuclear attack, then alas the policy of deterrence would have failed and we should be faced with disaster, our bluff would have been called. But the point is that our threat to use nuclear weapons is a bluff: it is not and never will be our intention to use these weapons. We must possess them because, alas, that is the kind of world in which we live. We can only preserve peace by remaining strong.'

This line of approach implies that the deterrent policy is based on a colossal lie and on that ground alone we may question its morality. But is it in any case a realistic proposition that a nuclear power, whatever its present intention may be, will *never* use the weapons upon which it has expended vast sums of money in the name of 'defence'?

'It may be true that, so long as rational counsels prevail, fear alone may suffice to prevent both sides from being the first to cast their stones. But it is too much to assume that rational counsels will prevail. The world provides all the opportunities for a "failure of nerve": an official or an individual failure of nerve. The tensions may well become near-intolerable; the temptation to put an end to them, to grasp what presents itself as a golden opportunity, may well sway official policies, and hysteria – and possibly even technical errors in interpreting radar-information – may easily bring about individual actions not countenanced by existing policies. The risks are incalculable.'[48] Indeed they are, and even more so if we are envisaging a situation in which nuclear war seems not just to be imminent but has actually been launched by an enemy. The risks are not just incalculable, but unacceptable.

The witness of the British Churches

In an earlier book I set out to explore the nature of morality. It is by no means a simple exercise. At the beginning I quoted from a much-discussed report entitled 'Sex and Morality' presented to the British Council of Churches in 1966:

'Is the (Christian moral) system to be thought of as valid for all men in all times and all places, because it is deduced from a divine revelation, through scripture and tradition, of man's true nature? Alternatively, is the Christian system of morality a 'dynamic' or 'evolutionary' system which has to be worked out afresh by each generation in the light of their own understanding of Christ, paying due regard to the conditions obtaining in their time and place? These two alternatives give us a striking, but over-simplified, picture of the present controversy over Christian morals as the advocates of the 'New Morality' tend to envisage it. Neither alternative completely represents a position we hold. Nevertheless we have assumed that new knowledge must be taken into account in arriving at a Christian moral judgement; and it could be asked, Is this really legitimate? Is not the Church officially and irrevocably committed to the doctrine of immutable moral rules?

In fact we have to deal with a number of separate questions of general principles . . . We may distinguish the following:

(i) Does morality derive from God's will or from man's judgement?
(ii) Is morality static or revisable?
(iii) Is it best embodied in rules or ideals?
(iv) Does it bear mainly on actions, or on motives and dispositions?
(v) How much liberty of interpretation rests with particular cultural groups or individuals?'[49]

My own general response to these important questions may be gathered from the following:

'The perpetual danger confronting the architects of our moral traditions has been the tendency to relapse into the kind of dead legalism which was rejected both by Jesus and St. Paul. During the seventh and eighth centuries we find that the use of "penetential books" was spreading. These were lists of sins with their appropriate ecclesiastical punishments. Later on they dealt with cases of conscience, and so laid the basis for the system of casuistry which was fully developed in the fourteenth and fifteenth centuries. Casuistry is the application of Christian principles to particular cases. It attempts to find the Christian "answer" in cases where the right way forward is in doubt, either because it is not clear how far a given law is binding on an individual in a certain set of circumstances, or because two laws appear to be in direct conflict.

'The present state of opinion in the Churches about the basis of moral judgement affords unprecedented opportunities for conversation of a sympathetic kind between Christians of different traditions. In particular, the closer relations between Protestants and Roman Catholics provide many occasions for fruitful dialogue. Protestants should be able to learn much from the past history and present-day discussions of moral questions in the Roman Church. The methods of detailed analysis employed by Roman Catholics have much to commend them but, as the past shows, the pitfalls of legalism abound. There is no escape for any of us from the necessity of casuistry defined as "the application of the principles of moral theology to individual cases". We are more likely to avoid mistakes in the present if we are well-informed about the errors of the past.'[50]

'The application of the principles of moral theology to individual cases' to which I refer imparts a dynamic quality to Christian morality. But if the perils of purely subjective judgements are to be avoided there must be a willingness to lean on the teaching authority of the Church, and, above all, to realize our dependence on the help and guidance of the Holy Spirit.

It will, therefore, be instructive to examine a series of quotations from the resolutions and reports of the British Council of Churches. Through all the years of the post-war period it has turned repeatedly to detailed consideration of the issues of peace, nuclear weaponry and disarmament. The Council represents the mainstream Churches of Great Britain. It has no authority to legislate for any or all of them. But its statements reflect responsible attitudes in all the Churches on many of the major issues of the day. This is particularly true of pronouncements on the matters with which we are dealing here. As is very evident, this is a field in which expert knowledge is of particular importance. The B.C.C. has been fortunate in being able to call on the services of exceptionally well-informed and well-equipped men and women in connection with the work of its Division of International Affairs. One of these, Mr. Sydney D. Bailey, has recently produced a summary entitled 'Christian Perspectives on Nuclear Weapons'.[51] This contains brief excerpts from statements received and resolutions endorsed by the

Council. They reflect not only a deepening concern, but a changing attitude to the questions with which they deal and in particular to the practical implications for British defence policy:

'"The argument that on balance the use of the atomic bomb saved hundreds of thousands of lives . . . undoubtedly has weight. But it is one of peculiar danger, since it can be used to justify any kind of barbarity" *Era of Atomic Power*, 1946, p. 50.

"The atomic bomb has so increased the scale of destructiveness that a single stroke, or a few successive blows, may annihilate the industrial capacity, and consequently the recuperative power, of the nation attacked . . . The incentive to strike a crippling blow first and the possibility of doing this are incalculably increased, and a premium is thus placed on swift ruthless agression . . . The use of atomic weapons makes war not only more destructive and treacherous, but more irresponsible than ever." *Era of Atomic Power*, 1946, pp. 10, 11, 12.

"A way out, within the western alliance for a start, may be found by placing nuclear weapons as they already exist under international control, that is, under the control of the alliance. It may not be possible for the U.S.A., in its unique position of power, to do this, but for Britain prudence and statesmanship may well continue to suggest such a step towards the ultimate goal." *Christians and Atomic War*, c.1959, p. 21.

"There would be a better chance of avoiding the spread of nuclear weapons to more and more nations if Britain, having had hers, gave them up or at least shared them with her allies. If it is unacceptable for Britain to surrender her megaton weapons, she might share control, and if possible, manufacture of them with her allies, or at least with America and France. This might help to stop the spread of nuclear weapons to further countries". *Valley of Decision*, c.1961, pp. 36, 39.

"The British Council of Churches
(i) records the profound concern felt by Christian people in Britain at the continuing experimental explosions of nuclear weapons, and at the grave danger which they may involve, by the increase of world radiation, for humanity as a whole;

(ii) deplores the decision of Her Majesty's Government to carry out a number of nuclear test explosions, in the megaton range, in the near future;

(iii) appeals to Her Majesty's Government, and to the Government of the U.S.A. and the U.S.S.R., to make a new and determined effort to secure a general nuclear control agreement as soon as possible, and in the meantime jointly to pledge themselves to refrain from any further tests of hydrogen bombs . . ." – *Resolution, 2–3*, April 1957.

"The Council believes that Britain should express her willingness to forego the claim to independent nuclear action if thereby more effective machinery can be established for the shared control of the deterrent in any part of the world and so the proliferation of national nuclear forces can be halted". – *Resolution of the British Council of Churches*, 16 October, 1963.

"The Council . . . believes that Britain . . .

(ii) should be prepared – if this would secure a satisfactory non-proliferation agreement – to forgo the possession of national nuclear weapons and to accept the same status as other non-nuclear allies in any use of nuclear weapons which the Alliance as a whole may judge to be necessary;

(iii) as a step towards international control and ultimate abolition, should strive for the restriction of the national possession of nuclear weapons to the Governments of the United States, the Soviet Union, and China." – *Resolution of the British Council of Churches*, 19 April 1967.

"The Assembly . . . believes that the non-replacement by the U.K. of its present nuclear strategic deterrent (with Polaris missile system) would strengthen moves for nuclear non-proliferation, and urges Her Majesty's Government to take a decision to this effect; invites other Governments to take comparable confidence-building measures of restraint or renunciation . . ." – *Resolution of the British Council of Churches*, 19 November 1979.

". . . The development and deployment of nuclear weapons has raised new and grave ethical questions for Christians. Because no gain from their use can possibly justify the annihilation they would bring about and because their effects on present and future generations would be totally indiscriminate as between military and civilians, to make use of the weapons would be directly contrary to the requirements of the so called just war . . .

The doctrine of deterrence based upon the prospect of mutual assured destruction is increasingly offensive to the Christian conscience." – *Resolution of the British Council of Churches*, 24 November 1980.'[51]

The various statements of the BCC reflect the corporate mind of the British Churches at the level of a responsible leadership which recognizes the complexity of the issues, and the inevitable compromise which is involved in any attempt to enter the field of political debate and decision. The Council has addressed its appeals to governments and has urged the need for multilateral action. As the arms race has continued to gather momentum, however, the need for unilateral initiatives has been more clearly recognized and stated. The resolution of 19 November 1979, calls upon the British government to abandon its independent nuclear force.

In a latter to *The Times* on the 21st October 1981 I made a point which I believe to be of great importance. It is an interesting fact that no-one wrote to contest what was written. The letter read:

'Sir, The tendency to don labels and to make black and white distinctions between what are seen to be opposing policies can sometimes obscure an important truth. The present polarization between those who espouse the cause of multilateral disarmament and those who plead for unilateral action is a case in point.

'In the aftermath of the tragic death of President Anwar Sadat many have praised his courage in making the historic journey to Jerusalem which initiated the Middle East "peace process". I myself travelled to Cairo nearly three years ago to present the annual peace award of the World Methodist Council to President Sadat. But that award was made in recognition of a unilateral action which, notwithstanding all the remaining threats to peace in the Middle East, opened up an era of new possibilities.

'The lesson of this is plain: there is little likelihood of progress on the multilateral front without some willingness to undertake unilateral initiatives. The test of real statesmanship today is the readiness to contrive and then to take the unilateral steps that will deliver us from the political impotence that allows the monstrous and idiotic arms race to escalate. Amidst all the ballyhoo of party conferences and political argument wise men will listen to discern where we are most likely to discover the leadership that such a time as this demands.'

The network of ecumenical contacts provides many opportunities for interchurch discussion and the development of broad-based consensus on the great global issues of the day. Having looked at some of the judgements emanating from the British Council of Churches I turn now to the most significant peace witness of the Christian Churches in the Netherlands, and to a recent approach made by them to the British Churches.

Testimony from the Netherlands

A letter from the Moderator and General Secretary of the Netherlands Reformed Church addressed to members of the British Council of Churches was received in the middle of 1981. It referred to the valuable work being done by the Netherlands Interchurch Peace Council. In response to a plea from that Council the Netherlands Reformed Church prepared an extensive report on nuclear arms. It went through six editions in seven months and was discussed at literally thousands of meetings in the parishes. Several hundred local study groups have been formed.

The letter from the Netherlands Reformed Church leaders asks that representatives from Holland should meet with representatives of the British Churches to discuss ways in which there can be wider cooperation in the tasks of peace. The British Council of Churches has responded warmly to this proposal and a consultation has been arranged to which it is hoped other European church leaders will also come. The British Churches are also considering the setting up of some kind of unit to coordinate the growing peace efforts of the British Churches and to offer guidance.

The General Synod of the Netherlands Reformed Church addressed a letter to all its congregations. Because it reflects so clearly the deepening Christian concern about the nuclear arms race and because of the challenge of its conclusions, I quote it in full:

'Christ is our peace. He showed us the way of peace by taking that road himself. In the community whose center is the crucified and risen Lord, we may seek one another out, hold one another firm and let our steps be directed in the path He has laid for us.

'This letter is written from the conviction that the present day arms race is a test of our obedience to our faith. In the face of the ever increasing build up and sophistication of nuclear destructive power in the world, the Church cannot remain silent. She cannot accept a situation in which peace continues to be maintained through an ever greater build up of the tools of destruction which within a matter of hours could deface and render the earth uninhabitable for thousands of years. Nor can the Church acquiesce in the fact that both East and West dedicate so many scarce natural resources and so much ingenuity to defending themselves against one another, that the fight against poverty and exploitation throughout the world remains perpetually subordinate.

'An extensive new discussion of the question of nuclear arms has been taking place in our Church. In this context we now wish the voice of the Synod to be heard. We are aware that we cannot speak in the name of all of you, but we wish to speak to you and thus with you.

'In the past thirty years, consecutive synods have warned against the continuing arms race with ever greater urgency. We now find ourselves at a point where many new developments have appeared which make this race even more unimaginably dangerous and frightening than before. In the next few years the number of nuclear weapons will again increase by thousands. The possibility for their military use are also increasing. The number of countries which have or which soon can have access to these weapons is steadily increasing. By human standards this can only lead to catastrophy, especially when we see the accumulation of points of conflict in so many parts of the world. In speaking about these developments, we realize that the sin which expresses itself here is deeply embedded within ourselves. We understand the present arms race as an expression of a far-reaching crisis in our culture in which there may be seen disobedience to God, failure to love our neighbours, an inclination to save ourselves at any price, and a reliance upon our own powers.

We call upon each other with urgency to communal repentance before God and to the confession of our corporate sin.

'At the same time we know that our own guilt, as individuals, as a church, and as a society, is not the final reality. Christ's Church lives by faith in her Lord who is victorious, not by means of violence or counter-violence but by suffering. She knows that, thanks to her Lord, enmity does not have the last word, and hears Him say: "All power both in heaven and earth has been given to me" (Math. 28:18). Through faith in the crucified and risen Lord the Church can live. Living upon the basis of this reality, she can offer resistance to those powers and forces which continue to look for answers to the world's conflicts in the threat of mass destruction.

'It is now eighteen years since the 1962 pastoral letter "On the Question of Nuclear Weapons" in which the Synod uttered a "No without any Yes" to nuclear arms. In that report nuclear weapons were considered unusable for any end to which armed force could legitimately be applied. Christians, it affirmed, whose consciences are bound to the world of God, would not be able to answer to their conscience for participation in a nuclear war, not even if the state demanded it of them. The Synod did not speak as unambiguously about the possession of nuclear weapons. The reason for this was not because a qualifying clause was added to the "No" which implied a "Yes" to the deterrent function of nuclear weapons, but because "abolition" of these weapons was not possible in the normal sense of the word; the question was, along what lines could the "No" be realized. In 1962, the Synod emphasized the importance of overcoming the atmosphere of mistrust, of the ministry or reconciliation, of the strengthening of international order and of a change of mentality. The precarious balance within the "community of fear" was understood to be an opportunity offered by God in His patience to us all to seek a solution and to form new relationships.

'We must now state that the way, which the Synod in 1962 hoped would prove to be a way out, has not been taken. On the contrary, the experience of the last eighteen years has shown us how the possession of these weapons has swept us along in their accelerated build-up and sophistication and in the development of a strategy of "limited" nuclear warfare. So, first of all, we must repeat our "No" of 1962 and then in all clarity state that this "No" also holds without qualification for the possession of all nuclear weapons. However, this repetition and clarification of our 1962 standpoint will not suffice. We also have to consider where we ourselves have fallen short. And we must dare to take another road.

'It is still the case that this "No without any Yes" can only be realized by way of a gradual process. But what process this must be and what decisions we must now make, given the seriousness of the situation, are questions more crucial than ever.

'We consider the call of the 1962 Synod to be of lasting importance and therefore wish to reaffirm it. At the same time, we assert that the road which has actually been taken, namely of simultaneous negotiation and further armament, has led to a calamitous proliferation of weapons. Of course we continue to hope for steps towards bilateral and multilateral disarmament. But at the same time we consider it necessary to plead for an approach in which negotiation goes hand in hand with steps which are already clearly set upon the road of disarmament. Since it has turned out to be impossible to reach multilateral decisions leading towards such steps, they should be taken unilaterally. They should be unambiguous in intention. They should not only point out the direction to be taken; they should also testify to a readiness to take that road ourselves. We consider (and this concerns our responsibility in our own society) that the denuclearisation of The Netherlands would be such an unambiguous step. We call for your support for this proposal.

'We are aware of the great dangers lurking in such a clear departure from what is continuously presented to us as self-evident. This is an unknown way. We believe, however, that there is no future in the present way of continuing to build up more and more sophisticated nuclear weapons.

'Religious freedom and freedom of speech are among the essential achievements of our society for which we are thankful. We have no illusions about political systems from which we wish to remain free and which we fear. But as believers we can say: we can live with our Lord no matter what the political system may be. In no case does the defence of our freedoms justify basing our security on the possible destruction of everything dear to us and to our opponents and on an assault on the creation.

'We realize that for all of us it will be very difficult actually to follow this new road. Therefore we plead for intensive dialogue at every level in our Church, in order that those who make our choice their own, and those who reject our choice, should render an account to one another of their deepest motives. In addition to this, in the near future, we intend to carry out an intensive discussion with those whose work directly involved them in this question, such as politicians, members of the armed forces, civil servants, and workers in certain industries. We shall have to enter into partnership with all those who, because of their direct involvement, will have to put their knowledge and insight in service of the search for a way out. In fact our politicians are now faced with decisions which are so extraordinary and so far-reaching that they need the prayers and the support of all of us, now more than ever. Our "No" to nuclear weapons and the choice this entails is made in the knowledge that God is merciful. If He does not show mercy upon us there will be no future. But if we pray for mercy and for a future, we must recognize that this involves obedience. Therefore we call upon the Church to listen to the word of the Lord and thereby to enter into a deeper fellowship with one another. In this present time of great danger for the whole of humanity, we look to the coming of Him, who says to His Church, "Do not fear; I am the first and the last, and the living One; and I was dead, and behold, I am alive for evermore, and I have the keys of death and of Hades." (Rev. 1:17/18).'

This letter which reflects realism, pastoral concern, profound faith and clear moral judgement, is important because it demonstrates how Christian thinking has developed over the increasingly dangerous years during which the arms race has continued to escalate in spite of efforts to halt the madness. Note the comprehensive approach and the logical progression of thought in the letter. It begins with Christ. That is where the Christian must always begin in the assessment of any issue. The arms race is seen as a test of Christian obedience: the credibility of the Church and its gospel will be measured by the response we make. Preparations for war are the more scandalous because they inhibit the fight against poverty. Christians are asked to recognise their share in the sin that perpetuates this evil state of affairs. But the power to overcome sin and evil is the gift of the risen Christ.

It is against the background of these fundamental beliefs that the letter goes on to reiterate the earlier condemnation of nuclear weapons issued by the Netherlands Reformed Church Synod, but then adds the unequivocal statement that the possession of nuclear weapons is also to be condemned. The Netherlands, whilst still pressing for multilateral disarmament should take a unilateral step, namely that of denuclearisation. This proposal is made with eyes wide open to possible consequences, but in the belief that if Christians are obedient, they have no need to fear. The letter ends with a declaration of the intention to pursue the way of intensive dialogue in the Church and between the Church and those who carry decision-making responsibilities in the political, military and industrial establishments.

None of the judgements made by the conciliar agencies of the Churches will satisfy all Christians. Some will feel that the public pronouncements do not go far enough, others that the call for unilateral action is dangerous and misguided. Nevertheless there is impressive evidence of convergence as more and more Christians of different traditions share in the continuing debate.

Judgements of the World Council of Churches

The judgements of the Churches in Great Britain and the Netherlands represent a growing consensus that is most fully reflected in the debates and deliverances of the World Council of Churches. The Council's Central Committee last met in Dresden in the German Democratic Republic from 16–26 August, 1981. Under the heading of 'Increased threats to peace and the tasks of the Churches' it adopted the following statements:

'I. The Central Committee of the World Council of Churches in August 1980 expressed its concern that "the gravest danger that humanity faces today is a nuclear holocaust". The Central Committee, meeting in Dresden in August 1981, painfully aware of the devastation caused by bombing during

World War II as tragically evidenced in this city and the continuing need to curb violence as a means of resolving international conflict, notes that international relations have deteriorated during the past year and have become even more dangerous. There has been intensification of tension and the emergence of disquieting trends:

(a) Concerted attempts to make acceptable new strategies concerning the feasibility of nuclear war, and tendencies to consider the possibility of a limited nuclear conflict in which victory is assumed to be possible. In particular we are disturbed by the development and production in various countries of new dehumanizing weapons. The neutron weapon is the most recent and obvious example. It is a tremendous threat because it makes the use of nuclear weapons more likely, even against less developed countries. It is a further incentive to escalate the arms race and therefore makes disarmament negotiations more difficult. Even at this stage we urge that the manufacture of this and any other weapons be stopped, that those already produced be eliminated and that no other nation decide to manufacture them.

(b) The inability, so far, to reach a positive conclusion to the post-Helsinki talks in Madrid on European Security and Cooperation reflects a deterioration in East-West relations which constitutes a setback to détente and a further obstacle to disarmament.

(c) The continuation of violent conflicts in areas mentioned in earlier statements of the Central Committee.

(d) The worsening economic crisis throughout the world with graver consequences for the poor nations resulting in tensions within and among nations.

(e) The continuing stalemate in the North-South discussions on global economic issues leading to confrontation and the reduction in aid to developing nations in contrast with the scandalous increase of expenditures on the arms race.

'II. The Central Committee of the World Council of Churches, recognizing that urgent steps are needed for the prevention of a nuclear war and for the de-escalation of regional conflicts, appeals to all political leaders in the following terms:

(a) The leaders of the two military blocs should meet at the earliest possible time to begin serious negotiations aimed at disarmament, both nuclear and conventional. To facilitate this process they and other national leaders should consider what unilateral steps for disarmament could responsibly be taken.

(b) The peace-keeping machinery of the United Nations and of regional organizations should be strengthened in the interest of confidence building and the settlement of disputes. Existing disarmament negotiations should be reactivated and intensified.

(c) In order to ease tension and build confidence among the nations, the nuclear powers should jointly propose a resolution in the United Nations Security Council which would give guarantees to countries which decide to create nuclear free zones that these will be fully respected.

(d) Adequate preparation at national and international levels to ensure the success of the second special session on disarmament of the United Nations General Assembly scheduled for mid-1982 is of the greatest importance.

(e) The widening economic gulf between developed and developing countries undermines confidence and is a threat to peace and cooperation. The industrialized nations should fulfil the United Nations goal for international development assistance and should start to negotiate in good faith for a more just relationship between the North and the South.

(f) The rights of people everywhere to seek changes in social, economic and political exploitative and unjust conditions must be supported.

'III. The Central Committee has in the past recommended to the churches a number of concrete actions for disarmament and against militarism and the arms race. In the light of the current, most dangerous situation, the Central Committee:

(a) Reaffirms the tasks and responsibilities of the churches in the context of the present exposure of humankind to the unprecedented risk of terrible and perhaps irreparable destruction.

(b) Emphasizes the need to state more clearly the basis of

involvement in the issues of war and peace in the context of struggle for justice.

(c) Emphasizes also the need to articulate the concerns for peace in clear, basic, firm affirmations.

(d) Calls upon the churches now to:

1) challenge the military and militaristic policies that lead to disastrous distortions of foreign policy, sapping the capacity of the nations of the world to deal with pressing economic and social problems which have become a paramount political issue of our times;

2) counter the trend to characterize those of other nations and ideologies as the "enemy" through the promotion of hatred and prejudice;

3) assist in de-mythologizing current doctrines of national security and elaborate new concepts of security based on justice and the rights of peoples;

4) grapple with the important theological issues posed by new developments related to war and peace and examine the challenges posed to traditional positions;

5) continue, according to the appeal contained in an earlier statement of the Central Committee, "to call attention to the root causes of war, mainly to economic justice, oppression and exploitation and to the consequences of increasing tension including further restriction of human rights".

(e) Commends the many member churches who have made renewed calls to peace-making, started, reactivated or intensified their efforts for peace, disarmament and against militarism and the arms race. This has included such useful initiatives as programmes of peace education and organization of events like "peace week" or "disarmament week".

(f) Calls upon member churches to:

1) intensify further their engagement in efforts for peace and join with others who seek to arouse the conscience of the public regarding the current threats to peace;

2) commit themselves to peace-making as continual witness through preaching, teaching and action;

3) promote bilateral and multilateral discussions among churches with a view to greater understanding among people

and the reduction of mutual distrust and fear.

(g) Commends the work of a large number of peace and disarmament groups and movements, old and new, around the world, in several of which large numbers of Christians actively participate in obedience to the demands of the gospel. We call attention to the plea of the Central Committee in Kingston that serious attention be paid to the rights of conscientious objectors.

(h) Commends to the churches the forthcoming W.C.C. International Public Hearing of Nuclear Weapons and Disarmament as an important occasion "to search for ways in which churches, Christian groups and others can help promote a climate of thinking more favourable to nuclear disarmament and for practical ways by which they can most effectively contribute to it".

(i) Urges the churches, in the context of preparations for the Sixth Assembly, whose theme is "Jesus Christ – the Life of the World", to make commitment to peace-making a special concern and to give emphasis to studies on issues related to peace, paying special attention to the underlying theological issues.'

The message of the Pope

The centrality of the search for peace for all who follow the way of Christ is a constantly recurring theme in the public utterances of the Pope. I end this chapter with a quotation from the message sent out by the Vatican in preparation for World Peace Sunday, January 1982:

'*Peace, a gift from God*

The theme chosen continues those on the preceding World Days and must be considered in the context of the Pope's journeys and the various discourses in which he has spoken of many aspects of peace.

'The theme is intended to stress God's intervention in our lives. "Unless the Lord builds the house, those who build it labour in vain. Unless the Lord watches over the city, the watchman stays awake in vain" (Ps 126 (127):1). This way of viewing things puts stress on the fact that it is only in the light of religious principles and the postulates of transcendence that man can reach full understanding of himself and others, and establish the common solidarity that is capable of creating well-ordered progress by human society through relationships by which people live together in truth, justice, love and freedom. From this point of view the specific contribution made by religion in general and the Church in particular to the cause of peace is supremely valid and illuminating. Any other view of the world and of the issues of peace, of such a kind as to ignore or deny man's orientation towards eternal realities, can never provide the nations with solid bases for a secure and truly lasting peace.

'The human race bears the marks of hatred, injustice, war and fratricidal terrorism, and religion reminds it that God created all human beings as brothers and sisters equal in nature and dignity. Furthermore, the Church recalls for Christians that "that earthly peace which arrives from love of neighbour symbolizes and results from the peace of Christ who comes forth from God the Father. For by his Cross the incarnate Son, the Prince of Peace, reconciled all human beings with God. By thus restoring the unity of all in one people . . . he slew hatred in his own flesh. After being lifted on high by his resurrection, he poured the Spirit of love into the hearts of men" (*Gaudium et Spes*, 78).

'Overcoming present difficulties between peoples through an openness to God in a unitary vision of the world that takes God as its point of departure and of arrival is the path that corresponds increasingly to the demands of the human spirit anxiously seeking valid solutions to the problems of peace in the world.

'Peace is a gift from God, since it is a "fruit of the Spirit" (Gal. 5:22), and it must be desired, prayed for, willed – and therefore merited – by each people and each individual.

'The theme also presents the occasion to stress the links between the great religions and the convergence between them. Faith in God, the basis for common action in favour of peace, unites them. And with regard to the advancement of peace among nations, it gives the opportunity to confront the position of those who, in theory or in practice, deny religious freedom with the position of those who see in that freedom the primary condition for effective action in favour of true peace.'

8: The making of peace

Blessed are the peacemakers.

The words of Jesus (Matthew 5:9)

It has been a basic contention of this book that the proper place for the Christian Church is at the heart of the current debate and in the leadership of the peace movement. The Church *is* God's peace movement. Some things, desirable in themselves, are optional for the Christian. Fasting is an example. There are no doubt many Christians who would greatly benefit from fasting for one day a week – or even two – but it is not obligatory. Or there is reading the New Testament in Greek. It is an admirable thing if you can do it, and a great aid to understanding the Bible, but you will not be kept out of heaven if you scarcely know the difference between alpha and omega. Peace-making, however, is different. It is not an optional extra. It is so central to the profession of a Christian that for a man to claim that he follows Christ, but is not interested in peacemaking, is as absurd as a baker who claims that he has nothing to do with making bread.

The primary purpose of this modest introduction to a huge subject will have been served if some readers reach this point asking 'What can I do?' In response to that question I offer some reflections under four headings: Participation; Sensitisation; Demonstration; Inspiration.

1. *Participation*

In the Introduction I referred to the sense of powerlessness felt by many people. I want to explore that point a little further. During the second half of the last decade the British Council of Churches embarked on a large project called 'Britain Today and Tomorrow'. Through expert working parties it sought to examine the British political, economic and social situation in depth and from a Christian standpoint. One of the working parties dealt with the subject of 'power and powerlessness'. The results of its enquiries were written up by Canon Trevor Beeson in one of the chapters of a book entitled 'Britain Today and Tomorrow'. In the chapter entitled 'The Decision Makers' the various centres of power within the nation are examined. It is recognized that in a complex society like ours it is not always easy to discover where power is actually located. Those who regularly watch the news on BBC and ITV must have wondered why these two quite independent channels seem most often to cover virtually the same topics and in identical order. The answer must be that they take their cue from the morning papers. Trevor Beeson rightly expresses concern that virtually all British newspapers are controlled by the most wealthy section of society, and are used to promote their interests.

We rightly cherish the freedom we enjoy compared with the situation of those who live under totalitarian regimes, but it is the existence of huge and powerful vested interests and of complex bureaucracies headed by 'faceless men' that induces in many people a sense of the futility of individual effort to affect the course of events. It is the business of Christians to seek in every possible way to encourage the creation of a truly participatory democracy. 'Britain Today and Tomorrow' states the matter thus:–

'Power is necessary to genuine freedom, therefore the power generated within a society must be distributed as widely as possible, not clung to by a minority, however capable or well-intentioned. Power must enable others, both individuals and communities, to grow in power and share in its exercise. Any over-concentration of power is not merely dangerous but unjust, and once established is notoriously hard to break up. In Britain today power is more widely shared than in some other parts of the world, but many people – including a high proportion of thoughtful Christians – believe that a further redistribution is needed, and that the abuse of power is still widespread and too easily tolerated.'[52]

The Churches have an important part to play in encouraging participation in public debate and decision-making. The B.C.C. Working Party on power and powerlessness acknowledged that the Churches themselves have much to learn about the subject from within their own structures. It is all too easy for systems of ecclesiastical government at every level, especially in a still male-dominated Church, to produce concentrations of power that inhibit individuals and discourage local initiatives. The aim of the Church must be to encourage individuals to participate, to formulate their own judgements, and to articulate them effectively. It belongs to the heart of the Christian message, with its stress on divine vocation, to insist that everyone counts and that each person has a unique part to play in God's unfolding strategy for His world.

But each member must also be encouraged to study the role of the Church and of the Churches in their corporate witness and activity. The idea of 'the godly remnant' is inseparable from the biblical understanding of both Jewish and Christian religion. So the psalmist in typical phrase sings of those whom God chose to be the instruments of His redemptive purposes: 'A small company it was, few in number.' (Psalm 105:12). History abounds in illustrations of what can be accomplished by well-informed and determined minorities. The movement to secure the right to vote for women was led by a handful of suffragettes. Once it would have seemed absurd to suggest that the slave trade could be abolished. But it happened and the fact that it did so may be largely attributed to a small group of dedicated enthusiasts. William Wilberforce, the great leader of the abolitionist movement, came out of retirement a few weeks before his death to address a public meeting. As he spoke his frail frame seemed to be rejuvenated. A gleam of sunshine suddenly lit up the hall. The old warrior caught it and wove it into his peroration. 'It is', he said, 'a light from heaven, an earnest of success'. E. M. Howse ends his fascinating account of the small group of earnest reformers, led by Wilberforce, called The Clapham Sect, with these words:—

'The Clapham Sect, in fact, did a great deal to change the atmosphere of the nation. Professor G. M. Trevelyan traces the origin of Victorian optimism in significant part to the anti-slavery triumph. "Mankind had been successfully lifted on to a higher plane by the energy of good men and the world breathed a more kindly air". Good had won such dazzling victories over such grim foes that multitudes of men were moved to a new faith in humanity, and a new confidence that almost any further victory might be possible. And that faith and confidence heartened the crusaders of the following generation. There was a fitting symbolism in the gleam of sunshine that lit up the last public words of Wilberforce. He and his faithful band had fought a weary battle under lowering skies. But at eventide there was light. They left England with an "earnest of success", and an awakened hope that days still brighter were to come.'[53]

Part of the problem of overcoming individual inertia and encouraging participatory democracy arises from the fact that when we take peacemaking seriously we are forced to grapple with very complex issues. That in turn compels us to consult the experts and then we discover that the experts do not always agree. As we saw in the second chapter, a very good example of this is the current debate about the peaceful uses of nuclear energy. How are we to judge the weight and value of conflicting evidence about the risks of radiation, accident, and the long-term storage and disposal of nuclear wastes? The temptation to 'leave it all to the experts' is very strong, but that temptation must be resisted. Peace is far too important to be left to the experts, whether they be scientists or politicians. In a democratic society the doctrine of accountability is of primary importance. This works two ways, however. Those who carry responsibility for making vital decisions must be subject to constant scrutiny and must endeavour to explain their policies in intelligible language. Far too much official communication consists of ladles full of a kind of alphabet soup lifted from a stockpot of esoteric verbiage. But there is also a responsibility which we ordinary citizens must exercise. It is partly a matter of maintaining that eternal vigilance upon which freedom depends; and partly a matter of intelligent effort to grapple with complex issues and understand them.

The need for participation in public debate lays upon the Churches an educational task which it is seeking to discharge through a variety of agencies, and particularly through the boards and departments of social responsibility. These agencies have among the various tasks assigned to them a two-fold function: on the one hand they act as the bridgeheads of the Churches into the kind of dialogue with the decision-makers which is so essential a part of true democracy; on the other hand they act as 'middlemen' seeking to convey in understandable language the information and the insights which enable Christians to reach sound conclusions. Neither part of this task is easy. I recall a number of occasions when a group representing the Churches has sat down with a government minister who has set out his case for a certain line of policy. Just as soon, however, as the Church representatives have raised the moral and theological questions which the exposition prompts in their minds, the reaction has been 'Ah well now, that is your sphere; I am not competent to enter into debate with you on matters of that kind'. Such a complete dichotomy is unacceptable to the Christian. The interpenetration of the world of affairs and the world of religion is a logical necessity if we proceed from the fundamental conviction that God has 'got the whole world in His hands'. Looked at from the standpoint of the Christian who is anxious to demonstrate the relevance of his faith the problem is scarcely less formidable. There have been times when I have been embarrassed by the self-confidence born of ignorance displayed by Christian spokesmen. Christians do not have a monopoly of moral concern, neither do they suppose that there are any ideal solutions to any contemporary problems. Compromise is an inevitable part of all the intercourse of nations and human communities of every kind.

The provisional character of the participatory exercise to which I have been referring is well stated at the end of a perceptive essay on the nature of Christian involvement in politics written by Alan Booth, a former director of Christian Aid:

'All our solutions are partial, contingent and temporary, a balance of advantages carefully struck and constantly renewed. None, in the Christian view, can represent the final meaning of our lives on earth. Indeed the greatest threat to human life in history perceived in the Jewish-Christian tradition is that involved in the attempt to find ultimate meaning in our political and social structures. This is the idolatry which in the end demands human sacrifice, the liquidation of men on the altar of ideology. We know this all too well in the twentieth century.

'But if there is no political and social structure which can

143

contain the meaning of our lives, there are certainly some which can betray and distort that meaning as we already recognise, and some which can create conditions in which our understanding of life's meaning can be enriched and enlarged. It is therefore one of the great functions of true religion in the political realm to present at every point a determined challenge to all absolutising of political philosophies and programmes, to expose the relative and provisional character of all political choices, and at the same time, with equal and even greater vigour, to provide the stimulus and conviction for men to pursue what is good in what is partial, temporary, and always incomplete. Religious sophistication is a dedication to that which is always beyond our apprehension in the terms of our life on this planet.'[54]

2. *Sensitization*

I have already referred to the remarkable influence of minority groups. The Church is a minority group. Jesus said (Matthew 21:21) that faith can move mountains. One description of the Church is 'the community of faith'. Both the words 'community' and 'faith' are important. Like many who will read these pages I can testify to the enormous difference it makes to belong to a fellowship of people all striving for a common goal. St. Paul refers a number of times to the task of 'edifying' (the root of the word is the same as that of edifice, a building) committed to the Church. The various offices in the Church are 'to equip God's people for work in his service to the building up (or edifying) of the body of Christ'. (Ephesians 4:11 and 12). This building up has many aspects. One undoubtedly is the encouragement that comes from sharing with others in a great enterprise based on a common faith. Another is the opportunities for honest self-examination, what I will describe as the sensitization of our consciences. Let us consider the need for that now.

Many of those who have written about the search for peace in the nuclear age have referred to what is called 'psychic numbing'. It is an emotional de-sensitization, a kind of anaesthetization of feeling, a reaction which shields people from the pain of being unable to cope. There are obviously great dangers in this tendency to avoid unpleasant facts, to look the other way, and to try to escape from thought and the painful feelings it provokes. A vacuum created by refusal to face the facts will quickly be filled. The words of Jesus may be applied here. If a man casts out of his heart 'the unclean spirit' of fear, but it is not replaced by positive commitment to the removal of the causes of fear, that unclean spirit will return. 'Off it goes and collects seven other spirits more wicked than itself, and they all come in and settle down; and in the end the man's plight is worse than before'. (Matthew 12:45).

Is there real evidence that the Churches are really in the forefront of the struggle for peace? Is there a vivid awareness of the importance and the centrality of the issue? Are we as members of Christ's Church stirring one another up to awareness and to the need to cooperate in a great and demanding effort? Honesty compels the answer that, although much is being done, apathy remains as the enemy of progress.

The Hiroshima bomb was dropped on the Feast of the Transfiguration, the day when Christians remember how Jesus went up a mountain with His disciples, Peter, James and John, and how the Master's 'face shone like the sun, and his clothes became white as the light' (Matthew 17:2). Peter's reaction was significant: he wanted to build shelters. But Jesus led His disciples down the mountain to the world in which they must face reality in the light of the truth He had revealed. On the Feast of the Transfiguration in 1945 there was a fierce white light over Hiroshima. It emanated from the most devilish device the sinful mind of man had ever produced. It was a light which could either blind men with terror, or reveal the enormity of our sin and the need for repentance ('change of mind'). In fact it produced a widespread psychic numbing.

It is the sense of repentance for our share in the sin which has brought us to where we are, and our sense of solidarity with all mankind that must motivate the Christian peacemaker, sensitizing his conscience and driving him to cooperate with others. But, I repeat, the confession of sin and the desire to repent must be given positive content by an honest attempt to examine how in fact we are affected and infected by sin. Sin is not an abstraction, it embodies itself in concrete attitudes and actions. In this task of self-examination we may be much helped by men like Dr. Nicholas Humphrey, the Assistant Director of the Department of Animal Behaviour at Cambridge. In October 1981 he delivered the third Bronowski Memorial Lecture entitled 'Four Minutes to Midnight'. He asked why we stand by and apparently do nothing to prevent the destruction of our world.

Dr. Humphrey argued that there are powerful inhibitory forces deflecting us from effective protest. He mentions four specifically. The first of these is *Incomprehension*. Faced with the grizly statistics about megatons and the possibility of millions of deaths we 'just can't take it in'. It is literally true. The mind boggles, that is to say it is like a simple calculator which is required to do an impossibly complex sum, far beyond its capacity. Often because we can't comprehend we just deny; we pretend to ourselves that it is all unreal and eventually actually persuade ourselves that 'it could never really happen'.

A second inhibitory factor is *embarrassment*. Few of us like to be embarrassed. It is amusing, yet revealing, to see how in a railway compartment, if a fellow-traveller indulges in some eccentricity like commenting aloud on the less attractive features of the ancient rolling-stock or even of the other passengers, the rest of the occupants tend to look out of the window as if nothing at all were happening. When it comes to nuclear weapons we tend to obviate our embarrassment by misusing language in the way we have observed in the course of our study. So the slaughter of whole populations is referred to as 'demographic targeting': a phrase to which the Archbishop of Canterbury took very strong exception in a speech he made at the Assembly of the British Council of Churches in November 1980. 'Demographic targeting' is merely a euphemism for 'mass murder'. It takes courage to be different, and anyone who reads the newspapers cannot but be aware of the fact that a whole vocabulary of clever denigration has been invented to mock at those who plead for disarmament. Perhaps the most damaging is the patronising allegation often made about 'well-intentioned but wholly unrealistic idealism'. If you don't want to be embarrassed, it is obviously best to keep quiet.

The third in Dr. Humphrey's list of inhibitory factors is the sense of *helplessness*, and to this I have already alluded.

His final reference is to what he calls *'the Strangelove Syndrome'*. This is a strange attachment to the engines of death, an attitude almost of welcome for the thing that is dreaded. I think that this not unfairly describes those to whose addiction to a certain understanding of apocalypse I referred in Chapter 6. They seem almost to glory in the prospect of imminent destruction.

Dr. Humphrey's incisive lecture (published in 'The Listener' of 29th October 1981) would make a very good basis for the kind of self-examination which both as individuals and as church communities we need frequently to undertake if we are to understand ourselves and be persuaded about the part that we can and must take in the struggle for peace. What I have described as sensitization is a vital part of the Church's ministry.

The concluding passage of the Lecture leads to my third heading.

3. *Demonstration*

'The Bomb is not an uncontrollable automaton, and we are not uncontrolling people.

'Our control lies – as it always has done *whenever it's been tried* – in the force of public argument and public anger. It was public opinion in this country which forced the ending of the slave trade – opinion marshalled then, as it can be now, by pamphlets, speeches and meetings in every village hall. It was fear of the public's outcry which prevented President Nixon from using an atom bomb in Vietnam, and it was the protests of the American people against that cruel and pointless war which eventually secured the American withdrawal. And now in Poland it is the people's loud support for free trade unions which is forcing changes on the reluctant Communist machine.

'We forget sometimes our own power. In this country every penny spent on armaments is money *we* subscribe, every acre of grass behind every barbed wire fence round every bomber base is an acre of *our* land, and every decision taken by every Minister of State is a decision made on our behalf by a representative elected to *our* service. If those we entrust to manage our affairs adopt strange policies: if they turn out, in office, to be double agents – one hand to pat our babies, the other raised in salute to the Bomb – then we have the right and the duty to dismiss them as unfit.

'What happens when an irresistible force meets a movable object? Why, it moves. But it will not happen quietly.

'Dylan Thomas spoke these words to his ageing father:

Do not go gentle into that good night.
Rage, rage against the dying of the light.'[55]

The central thrust of the passage just quoted is that the major hope of a turn towards sanity lies, to quote my own words at the beginning of our study, in 'a great popular uprising of ordinary people the world over'. We must now consider that judgement more carefully and respond to the sort of objections that might be raised against it by Christians. Those objections usually run something like this: 'What you are advocating is an entirely humanistic approach to the problem. Dr. Humphreys, whom you quote with approval, did not deliver his lecture from any Christian text, and seemed to be suggesting that we can pull ourselves up by our own shoe-straps. The hope which he expounds is a secular hope and there is really no such thing. The Christian hope is something entirely different, and is founded on what God has done in Christ and not on anything unaided man can do. In any case, demonstration is an entirely inappropriate activity for Christians. Moreover there is the gravest danger of our finding ourselves mixing with extremists, and even of being taken for a ride by the Communists. No, demos and protest marches have no place in the programme of the Christian peacemaker'.

There are a number of related points in this objection to which I want to respond.

First of all, and quite simply, what matters in any man's utterance is not the credentials to which he lays claim but rather whether what he says is true or false. Jesus Himself said 'He who is not against us is on our side' (Mark 9:39). Christians are often put to shame when they hear unbelievers stating the demands of the gospel more clearly than they do themselves. It is perfectly true that a world freed from the evil of war, and nations delivered from the awful incubus of astronomical expenditure on arms, is not the whole of the

Christian hope, for that hope is multi-faceted and embraces this life and the next, time and eternity. But Christians are right to hope for that for which they constantly pray in the name of Christ – 'peace in our time'.

Not only so, but the prayer for peace must be accompanied by a commitment to seeking peace. It would be sheer hypocrisy to pray constantly that God will relieve the wants of the poor and abolish hunger from the earth – and do nothing about it. The same is true of peace. The Apostle who urged his fellow-Christians to 'pray continually' (1 Thessalonians 5:16) also talked about our being fellow-workers 'sharing in God's work' (2 Corinithians 6:1). Since, then, the intention of God is plainly declared in the song of the angels at the birth of Christ – 'on earth his peace, his favour towards men' (Luke 2:14) – we are called to share in the task of building peace. By the same token we must oppose that which threatens peace. If that be accepted, then inevitably as Christians we are plunged into the never-ceasing discussion of how God would have us operate in response to His mandate.

I can find nothing in the gospel which would preclude me as a Christian from working with those who share with me a passionate desire for peace while unable to accept the Christian creed as I understand it. On the contrary I find every encouragement to make common cause with all who have a care for truth and a similar perception of the evils which afflict mankind.

This does not mean that any and every 'peace activity' has a proper claim on my support. Quite apart from the fact that there are so many peace movements and I must therefore be selective in the support I can give, some employ methods that I deem to be inconsistent with the profession of a Christian. There is, obviously, a basic contradiction in the activities of those movements which seek to establish peace by the use of violence, whether of a physical kind, or through the denial of the right of free speech to the others.

What of the danger that Christians will find themselves consorting with 'extremists'? It is not one, I believe, which should trouble us unduly. Our Lord was criticised for the strange company He kept. In any case, who are the extremists? What could be more extreme than defence policies based on the notion of mutual assured destruction?

Christians must, of course, be vigilant, and the policies and programmes of the peace movements must be subject to constant scrutiny in the light of our shared understanding of the will of God. Allegations have been made – usually without substantiating evidence – that peace movements in Britain are supported by money from the Soviet Government. We must always be in a position to be able to rebutt suggestions of this kind.

Precisely how the individual Christian is to contribute to the urgent task of peace-making must be a personal decision. For my part I want to see the members of the Churches providing a much stronger element within the recognised peace movements, not only because that support is needed but also because specific commitment to a cause strengthens conviction. To lay your beliefs on the line, to articulate them in the face of opposition and openly to declare them is the surest way both of discovering what you really believe and of believing it more firmly.

One way or another, then, so I urge, the Churches and their members must demonstrate their commitment to peace. During the year when I was President of the Methodist Conference in Great Britain I wrote an open letter to the Methodist people. The privilege of leading them for one year obviously presents opportunities denied to one in a more limited ministry. In the letter I set out some of the facts about the arms race, ventured some opinions, and appealed for a response. In particular I urged the members of my Church to support the World Disarmament Campaign. This Campaign aims at collecting millions of signatures to a petition to be presented to the United Nations Special Assembly on Disarmament in 1982 in order to demonstrate how widespread is the public concern about the arms race. The petition reads as follows:

'PETITION: To all Governments and to the United Nations General Assembly Special Session on Disarmament, 1982:–
    We, the Peoples of the World, demand:–
    1. The Abolition of Nuclear Weapons and all Weapons of Mass Destruction.
    2. The Abolition, by agreed stages, of Conventional Arms, leading to

3. General and Complete Disarmament
4. Transference of Military Expenditure to end World Poverty.'

But it is so general as to mean Nothing.

The response to my appeal was both moving and encouraging. Large numbers of Methodists trudged from door to door with the petition as did many other supporters of the Campaign in and beyond the other Churches. It is hoped that the presentation of the petition will itself have some effect on those who represent the nations at the U.N. Special Assembly. Perhaps even more important is the fact that through this Campaign much useful educational work is being done, men and women are being asked to think and think again, and many people have been brought to a deeper personal commitment to the cause of peace.

There are many other movements that provide opportunities for demonstrating a desire to contribute to active peace-making. The National Peace Council, 29 Great James Street, London, W.C.1. can supply a lengthy list of such organisations. Housman's Book Shop, 5 Caledonian Road, London, N.1. sells an Annual Peace Diary which contains information about both national and international peace groups. Some of the best-known of these are The Fellowship of Reconciliation, Pax Christi, the Peace Pledge Union, the United Nations Association, the Campaign for Nuclear Disarmament and the Women's International League for Peace and Freedom. Some of the peace organisations are pacifist, others not; some have a religious and others a humanist base. They are all concerned to promote education in the facts of our present situation and to stir people to active concern.

Very many of us are involved in all kinds of organisations which embrace an educational aim. Schools, social clubs, trade union branches, professional associations, as well as the multifarious meetings and programmes run by Churches, all provide opportunities for discussion of peace and disarmament issues and education in the facts.

The important thing for each individual is to begin somewhere. The first step will always lead to others. There is no-one who cannot make some contribution to a cause the importance of which it would be impossible to exaggerate.

4. *Inspiration*

One day in October 1981 I had the privilege of speaking at the ceremony in London at which the annual peace award of the World Methodist Council was made to Lord Soper. This award was established several years ago as a symbol of commitment to the cause of peace and to enable the Methodists of the world to pay tribute each year to someone who has rendered distinguished service to that cause. On a previous occasion I presented the award to Miss Sadie Patterson a remarkable lady who has lived all her life in the Shankhill Road, Belfast. She has devoted herself to the building of bridges of friendship between the conflicting sides in that deeply-divided country. She has not been daunted by defeat and her example of Christian courage and persistence has been a shining light in a dark place.

Reference has already been made to the award to President Anwar Sadat in December 1978 (see p. 152). This was made the occasion of a national event and he himself was visibly moved at this gesture of friendship offered to a Muslim leader by a Christian Community.

When the award was made to Lord Soper for 'courage, creativity and consistency' in pursuit of peace I was glad to testify to my own personal knowledge of the way in which that noble minister of the gospel has exemplified those qualities, and not least the last of them. He has never shunned controversy and has frequently been under attack. Never once in more than forty years have I known him to lose his equanimity and the fundamentally eirenic quality which is the hallmark of his greatness. Moreover the other side of the public controversialist is a man of humble devotion to the Lord who is the source of his strength and beneath whose cross he daily stands.

I make these comments because the way of the peacemaker is hard and demanding. We need inspiration if we are to stay the course. St. Paul says we are to 'pursue the things that make for peace'. (Romans 14:19). Thus we are reminded that if we engage ourselves to search for peace it is a lifetime's pursuit. For peace is not some condition which exists on its own. We have to pursue 'the things that make for peace' and we know from our study what they are. There is, in particular, justice and all that that involves: a more equitable distribution of the earth's resources, the removal of all kinds of discrimination, the creation of structures which enable people to live with dignity and mutual respect, confidence-building measures, and so much more. It is a long, hard road.

I am, therefore, glad to acknowledge some of those who have inspired me in the quest for peace. There are many more whom I have met only in their writings, like Martin Luther King and Mahatma Gandhi. Both of these, like Anwar Sadat, were killed, which reminds us just how hard the way of the peacemaker can be. I can remember the precise spot on a road in South Wales where I was when the news of Gandhi's assassination came over the car radio. As to millions of others, it seemed to me as if a light had suddenly been turned off. I treasure among my records a disc containing a speech delivered by Martin Luther King just before he died. It was given to me at an American University where I was speaking from the very platform he had used a couple of weeks before. He was late arriving for his appointment. In apologising he said with typical humour, 'I said to the young driver who was dashing me to the campus, "Slow down: I would rather be Martin Luther King late than the late Martin Luther King"'. Very soon he was to be just that. But the speech is full of faith and rings with that inspiring vision of a world ruled by Christ the King, a world of justice, brotherhood and peace.

Peter D. Bishop has written a most readable account of the methods of non-violent resistance developed by Gandhi and King from their different religious beliefs. I believe with him that the Churches should give much more thought to this concept. Bishop concludes his study with this suggestive paragraph:

'The possibilities of non-violent resistance are great, and still largely unexplored. In perilous times we would do well to heed the teaching and example of Mahatma Gandhi and the adaptation of his work by Martin Luther King Jr. They have given the world remarkable demonstrations of a technique for loving; a technique which resolutely seeks justice, but also desires only good for those against whom the struggle is carried out and works for the ultimate benefit of friend and foe alike; a technique which speaks in the positive phrases of cooperation rather than the negative tones of confrontation; a technique which demands of its users much courage, tenacity and sensitivity; and a technique which blends in an unusually effective way moral and spiritual insights from East and West.'[56]

As I have hinted, every public man has a private side. From whence comes the inspiration that keeps a man true to his vocation as a peacemaker right to the end of the journey? The example of others helps enormously, as I have said, but for the Christian there is something more. The secret of the peace-filled life is companionship with Christ, the One who said, 'Peace is my parting gift to you, my own peace, such as the world cannot give'. (John 14:27).

This inner peace, a centre of stillness at the core of one's being is indeed a gift. It cannot be earned, or bought, but the secret of how it may be received and retained is an open one. It is given to those who commit themselves in faith to Jesus Christ. What does that mean? It is so easy to use the kind of language that religious people understand, or imagine that they do, but which for others is opaque so that the secret of our inner peace remains a secret. Let me then state the matter in a different way, more in terms with which we are all familiar.

Commitment to Christ is in part a matter of admiring Him. There is more to it than that, but admiration (which can be very close to worship) will do for a start. And we all have people whom we admire. When I was still a boy a silvery-haired preacher came to talk to a group to which I belonged. After all these years I still remember his theme. 'Tell me', he said, 'whom you most admire and I will tell you what sort of person you are'. It is a good test, maybe a disturbing one. If we admire most of all those whose strength is expressed in gentleness, it will reveal much about ourselves, for we tend to become like those whom we consistently admire.

Christian commitment, which is the source of inner peace, requires the assent of the mind and heart, but no-one can achieve it on his or her own. There are three things, in particular, that help and inspire. One is to join with others who are seeking to know and follow Christ. That is what the Church is for: it is on one sense like a comprehensive school, and it is very comprehensive indeed, embracing some who have gone a long way in the direction of learning about Jesus

Christ, and others who have barely begun.

The second aid to commitment and source of inspiration is the Bible. Its power over the minds of men and women down the ages is an amazing phenomenon. Its dream of peace, expressed in language of breath-taking beauty, has inspired generations of peacemakers. The picture language of Isaiah is an example:

'Then the wolf shall live with the sheep,
and the leopard lie down with the kid;
the calf and the young lion shall grow up together,
and a little child shall lead them;
the cow and the bear shall be friends,
and their young shall lie down together.
The lion shall eat straw like cattle;
the infant shall play over the hole of the cobra,
and the young child shall dance over the viper's nest.
They shall not hurt or destroy in all my holy mountain'.
(Isaiah 11:6–9)

The focal point of the Bible is Jesus Christ. On my old college campus all paths lead to the chapel. So in the Bible all the prophetic fingers point to Christ and the road taken by the long line of witnesses stretching across two thousand years goes back to Him. Christians often refer to the Bible as 'the Word of God'. It is a strange description. But, then, a word is a strange entity. It is a collection of letters which can be conveyed in a sound or in written signs; but, much more important, it is the articulation of a thought. Thought is the mainspring of all motive and action. Because man is a thinking animal he is much more than an animal, he is human. One of the most profound statements in the Bible is 'The Word became flesh' (John 1:14). The Word is the Thought that caused all things to be: just as some marvellous tapestry once existed only in the thought of the artist who made it, so the creation came out of the thought of the Creator. But the God who thinks thus creatively, when He came to earth became a man, not an animal: the flesh referred to was human flesh. It had to be because only a thinker can know a thinker. The Bible reveals the thoughts of God so we are able 'to think God's thoughts after Him'. We know Him to be, as the great collect for peace says, 'the author of peace and lover of concord'. At the heart of the Bible is the benediction pronounced on those who are inspired by God's thought: 'Blessed are the peacemakers'. (Matthew 5:9).

Finally there is the help and inspiration of prayer. The point about prayer is that it is a very natural thing and, at the same time, it is supernatural as well. It is natural in the sense that all kinds of people pray, often in those unguarded moments when we just 'do the thing that comes naturally'. Prayer is often sparked off by a sudden sense of need or danger. Then the dividing wall between 'natural' and 'supernatural' becomes only paper thick.

The Church encourages Christians to pray and to engage in some discipline of prayer. It's rather like athletics (and St. Paul sometimes uses the imagery of the athlete) – most of us can run, but if we get into training we shall run more effectively and be able to carry off a prize. The liturgies of the Church help Christians to pray regularly, intelligently and meaningfully. There is something inspiring about the chain of prayer which binds one generation to another. In some ancient Churches the prayers seem almost to have sunk into the stonework so that a strong silence emanates from them with the force of a real but unseen presence.

While I have been writing these chapters I have been involved in the launching of the 'Prayer for Peace'. The original discussions which led to its launching in Westminster Abbey on Hiroshima Day 1981, took place in the home of the Dean of Westminster. Representatives of the British Churches shared with friends from the Jewish, Hindu, Jain, Buddhist, Sikh and Baha'i faiths. There was no attempt to disguise our very different understandings of God and religion, but one thing we all shared: the practice of prayer and the desire to pray for peace.

Details about the Prayer for Peace can be obtained from 21 Little Russell Street, London, W.C.1. It has gone out to the ends of the earth. The aim is to get millions of people using the same prayer at noon each day. Those who undertake to do so may often forget. It matters not: it is always noon somewhere on the face of the earth.

The human and psychological effect, in a world drenched in violence, of millions of people praying positively each day for peace could be considerable. But more important than that, though related to it, is the fact that prayer for peace is intended to make us instruments of the divine will, people through whom God Himself can act.

Here, then, is the prayer for the makers of peace:

'Lead me from death to life, from falsehood to truth,
lead me from despair to hope, from fear to trust,
lead me from hate to love, from war to peace,
let peace fill our heart, our world, our universe.'

References

1. *Effects of Nuclear War* U.S. Arms Control and Disarmament Agency, April 1979.
2. *Apocalypse Now?* 1980. Lords Mountbatten, Noel Baker and Zuckerman. pp. 13–14.
3. *Anticipation* published by World Council of Churches, June 1979, p. 36.
4. *From Hiroshima to Harrisburg* 1980. Jim Garrison.
5. *Shaping Tomorrow* published by Home Mission Division of the Methodist Church, 1981.
6. *The Times* 26th September, 1981.
7. *Nuclear Crisis* edited by David Gosling and Hugh Montefiore, 1977.
8. *North-South: A Programme for Survival* The Brandt Report, 1980, p. 162.
9. *The Waste Makers* Vance Packard. Longmans 1960. p. 47.
10. *The Psychology of Military Incompetence* Norman F. Dixon. Futura Publications Ltd. 1979.
11. ibid p. 20.
12. ibid p. 21.
13. *World Military and Social Expenditures 1980* Ruth Leger Sivard. World Priorities, 1980.
14. ibid pp. 15 and 16.
15. *Protest and Survive* Ed. by E. P. Thompson and Dan Smith. Penguin Books, 1980, pp. 218–19.
16. *World Military and Social Expenditures 1980* p. 10.
17. *The Arms Bazaar* Anthony Sampson. Hodder & Stoughton 1977, p. 338.
18. *The Neutron Bomb* Eric Burhop. Campaign for Nuclear Disarmament. 3rd edition. 1981, p. 14.
19. *Britain and Nuclear Weapons* Lawrence Freedman, The Royal Institute of International Affairs, 1980. pp. xii –xiv.

20. *The Game of Disarmament* Alva Myrdal. Spokesman 1976, pp. 15 and 16.
21. *A Farewell to Arms* Elizabeth Young. Penguin 1972, p. 135.
22. *Approaches to Disarmament* Nicholas A. Sims. Quaker Peace Service, 1979, p. 52.
23. ibid, p. 110.
24. *How Nations Behave: Law and Foreign Policy* Pall Mall Press for the Council on Foreign Relations, 1968, p. 182.
25. *Approaches to Disarmament* Nicholas A. Sims. pp. 48 and 49.
26. ibid. p. 76.
27. *The Game of Disarmament* Alva Myrdal, p. 120.
28. *Life in All its Fullness* Philip Potter, World Council of Churches 1981, p. 84.
29. *The Brandt Report* pp. 312.
30. *Geography of Hunger* Josué de Castro. p. 31, Gollancz, 1953.
31. *Our Crowded Planet* Fairfield Osborn. Allen and Unwin, 1963, p. 157.
32. *The Population Explosion* Richard M. Fagley. O.U.P. 1960, p. 47.
33. *The Brandt Report* pp. 78–9.
34. *Famine – 1975!* William and Paul Paddock. Weidenfeld & Nicholson, 1968, p. 206.
35. ibid pp. 207–8.
36. *Small is Beautiful* E. F. Schumacher. Sphere Books, 1974, p. 143.
37. ibid pp. 146–7.
38. *The Brandt Report* p. 282.
39. *The Brandt Report* p. 284.
40. *The 1980's: Countdown to Armaggedon* Hal Lindsey, Bantam Books, 1981, p. 4.
41. *On Being a Christian* Hans Küng. Collins 1978, pp. 219–20.
42. *Declarations of the Methodist Church on Social Questions* Epworth, 1959, pp. 52–4.
43. *The Foundations of Peace in Europe* Lord Carrington. Foreign and Commonwealth Office, London, 1981, pp. 5–7.

44. *Race to the Finish* Dervla Murphy. John Murray, 1981. pp. 196–7.
45. *The Politics of Uranium* Norman Moss. Andre Deutsch 1981, p. 201.
46. *Prospects for Peace* Frank Barnaby. Pergamon Press, 1980, p. 44.
47. ibid p. 47.
48. *Nuclear Weapons and Christian Conscience* ed. by Walter Stein. Merlin Press 1961, p. 74.
49. *Sex and Morality* SCM Press 1966, p. 17.
50. *The Art of Moral Judgement* Kenneth G. Greet. Epworth Press 1970, pp. 69–70 and 71.
51. *Christian Perspectives on Nuclear Weapons* B.C.C. 1981.
52. *Britain Today and Tomorrow* Trevor Beeson. Collins 1978. p. 178.
53. *Saints in Politics* Ernest Marshall Howse. Allen & Unwin, 1953, p. 185.
54. *Not only Peace* Alan Booth. SCM Press 1967, p. 140.
55. *Four Minutes to Midnight* The 1981 Bronowski Memorial Lecture. Quoted from The Listener of 29th October, 1981.
56. *A Technique for Loving* Peter D. Bishop. SCM Press, 1981, p. 158.

Incredibly little on how politics actually work.